LIGHT REALIZED

LIGHT REALIZED

* * *

LIVING THE

REALIZATION

* * *

A GUIDE TO LIVING FROM
THE LIGHT WITHIN

* * *

JARED RICHEY

Cover design: Wesley Miller & Lynna McMillon
Interior design: Jared Richey
Editorial assistance: ChatGPT (OpenAI)

ISBN: 979-8-9939613-0-9

This book is a work of spiritual reflection. It is intended to inspire, encourage, and invite contemplation. It is not intended to offer medical, psychological, or legal advice.

For more information, visit: **www.LightRealizedPress.com**

*To the Source of all things, the Spirit who guides
me, and the Light & Truth
who has set me free.*

Author's Note

Light Realized was written knowing that everyone's spiritual journey is exclusively their own, but there are moments when we share the same paths along the way.

In those moments, we glimpse the unity behind our individuality, the One Light expressing itself through countless reflections. May these words serve as gentle mirrors, reminding you of what has always been within you: wholeness, awareness, and peace.

—Jared Richey

CONTENTS

Acknowledgments

First, I want to thank my amazing wife, Tracie, my wonderful son, Ryker, and my beautiful daughter, Roxey, for your love, support, patience, and the space you gave me while this book took shape. You carried more than you know, and I am deeply grateful.

I'm also thankful for my mother and siblings; each of you help shape the way I see the world by consistently pointing out the good in people and in situations, even when it would have been easier to focus on the negative.

To the colleagues and friends who have shared countless in-depth conversations with me over the years: thank you. Many of the insights in these pages were refined through honest dialogue; through listening, questioning, and seeking together.

And to the many teachers, writers, researchers, and encouragers who have given their time and work to help spread truth and love, thank you. "You will know them by their fruits." Your fruit has nourished and strengthened my journey, and it continues to inspire me.

With gratitude, I want to recognize the influence of voices such as: John Burke, Eckhart Tolle, Joe Dispenza, Dr. Gary Schwartz, John Mark Comer, Ronalafae Thapa, Roger Lightfeather-AKA-Grandfather, Patrick Morley, Richard J. Foster, Nick "Sunshine" Tokman, Betty J. Eadie, Kimberly Klein, Talia Klein, Paul Miller, Don Miguel Ruiz, Lynne McTaggart, Suzanne Giesemann, John Eldredge, Gary Chapman, Charles Stanley, Craig Groeschel, Carter Conlon, Ken Harrison, Regi Campbell, Carlos Walker, John Calvert, Roy Mills, Stephen Mansfield, Randy Alcorn, Dr. Kenneth Ring, Luke Healy and many others.

Finally, to every reader—thank you for choosing to take this journey. My hope is simple: that these pages help you remember what has been true all along, and give you practical ways to live from that Light.

— Jared Richey

Introduction

As a child, perhaps you sang the song, "This little light of mine, I'm gonna let it shine..." or have heard it at some point in your life. The lyrics have shifted over its hundred-year history, but the heart of the song still carries a simple truth:

There is a light within you.
And that light is not just yours.
It is the Light within all.

I write this book with deep respect for every reader; Christian, Hindu, Muslim, Buddhist, Sikh, Spiritualist, Atheist, unsure, searching, or "none of the above." Beyond belief and difference lies a deeper reality: the light of our shared humanity. We stand or fall together, and only through love, understanding, and compassion can we, and the Earth that sustains us, truly flourish. Light Realized is about waking up to that Light.

A Gentle Request as You Read

Many people hesitate to read or consider someone's writings if they don't align 100% with what they already believe. I understand that. I did that for years.

We fear that if we listen to anything outside our familiar framework, we might be "led astray," or that it somehow dishonors Scripture or our tradition. But if the God we trust is real and present, then truth is never something we have to fear. Scripture itself reminds us:

- that God is always with us,
- that the Spirit guides us into truth,
- and that wisdom has been spoken through very imperfect people.

The writers of Scripture were not flawless. They wrestled, doubted, failed, and made painful mistakes, yet they were still beautifully used to share truth, guidance, and wisdom. If God could speak through them in all their humanity, then surely God can also use the reflections, research, and imperfect words of ordinary people today—not as new Scripture, but as additional light on the path.

We do ourselves and others a disservice when we refuse to even *consider* someone's insights just because they come from a different tradition, vocabulary, or angle than we're used to. If the foundations of our beliefs are shaken by another person's perspective, the invitation is not to panic and shut down, but to look carefully and honestly at the cracks that appear:

- *What exactly is being shaken?*
- *Is it the living foundation—or a layer of conditioning I've never really questioned?*
- *Am I listening with my heart or my head?*

If your foundation is true, honest questioning will only make it stronger.

Throughout my spiritual journey, whenever I've encountered truth, it has spoken to something deeper than my opinions; it speaks to my heart and soul. I believe that is where we are called to listen from, rather than from a conditioned mind. In the end, your heart is a truer filter for truth than your head.

I am not offering this book as a new authority, but as one person's honest journey with God, filtered through Scripture, experience, study, and a lot of stumbling. You are absolutely free to disagree with anything you read here. My invitation is simply this: don't shut your heart before you've even listened.

I invite you to widen your perception and loosen the boundaries; both the ones the world has imposed and the ones you've built within yourself. Society's expectations can become invisible bars, confining the mind and shrinking the soul's sense of possibility. But growth is not an accident; it is a sacred opportunity...your spirit learning to expand through contrast, limitation, and choice.

What if part of our purpose on Earth is not to reach Heaven as a far-off reward, but to reveal Heaven here and now?

"Your kingdom come, Your will be done on earth as it is in heaven."

Why Light Realized?

The title points to a simple but life-changing truth: you are not trying to get more of God...you are waking up to the Presence that has never been absent.

Jesus said, "I am the light of the world" (John 8:12), and then turned to ordinary, imperfect people and said, "You are the light of the world" (Matthew 5:14). Both are true.

Light Realized explores what happens when that truth moves from a belief in your head to a realization in your heart; when you stop living as a fearful-separate self, searching for the Divine "out there" and begin to live as someone already held, indwelt, and surrounded by Love "right here."

"Realized" doesn't mean you suddenly become flawless. It means the lights come on. You begin to see who you are, who God is, and what life is in a new way. Grace is offered through the totality of *tetelestai*—"it is finished"—a work completed eternally, backward and forward. Saying yes to that Grace leads into the fullness of life God always intended for His creation.

Many Names, One Presence

Different people use different names for the same reality: God, Source, Love, Christ, Creator, Spirit, the I AM, the Light, the Universe.

Every name has been shaped by culture and time, but no word can fully contain the Infinite. Language is a bridge, not a boundary. The mystic, the scientist, the preacher, the poet, and the child may describe their encounter differently; but what matters is not the name, but the knowing.

Throughout this book, you'll see Scripture because it is the language of my heart. You'll also see near-death testimonies, neuroscience, and modern research into consciousness—not to replace Scripture, but to show how again and again, honest inquiry and lived experience point toward the same core reality: a Living Presence of love and truth at the center of everything.

Who This Book Is For

This book is for you if:

- You're tired of anxiety, fear, and worry dictating how you move through your days.
- You want to live from your true heart, not just from survival mode or inherited fear.
- You believe in God (or something beyond yourself) but the way you've been taught to see the Divine still leaves you afraid, ashamed, or uncertain.
- You long for a faith that can hold both mystery and reason, Scripture and science, devotion and honest questions.

All truth is God's truth. The Light is not threatened by sincere searching.

Whether you are devout, deconstructing, more spiritual than religious, skeptical, or simply curious, if you carry a longing for what is authentic and whole, you are welcome here.

How to Read This Book

This is not a book to sprint through. Read it slowly. Pause when a sentence tugs at you. Sit with the questions. Pray, ponder, or simply be still. And if you disagree, bring that disagreement into conversation with God. He is not fragile.

Let these pages be a dialogue between your heart and the Heart that made you. The goal is not to give you more information, but to help you recognize the Presence already moving through your life.

A Final Word Before We Begin

My hope is simple: That as you read, something in you will quietly say, "Yes. This is what I've known all along."

You are loved. You are held. You are not separate from God. And the Light you've been seeking? It has been seeking you all along.

Let's begin.

PART I—THE AWAKENING

Remembering What Has Always Been True

Awakening does not begin with mastering spiritual concepts; it begins with a whisper. Something in you quietly realizes, *"The life I've been living is too small for the truth I carry."* Part I traces that sacred shift; from the first inner nudge to the lived experience of a new way of being.

In Chapter 1, you hear the call to wakefulness: the ache that says, "There is more," and the first recognition that the kingdom is within you. Chapter 2 invites you to see with new eyes—to recognize life as symbolic, patterned, and deeply connected, a living conversation between you and God. In Chapter 3, sight begins to ask something of your choices, and alignment emerges: your inner knowing and outer life slowly start to walk together. Finally, Chapter 4 explores embodiment; truth moving from idea to identity, as presence, balance, and love become the atmosphere you live in, not just moments you visit.

Part I is the beginning of remembering: not becoming someone new, but waking up to who you have always been in the Light.

Throughout this book, you'll find italicized questions. Let them slow you down. If one tugs at you, sit with it; there's light there.

.

CHAPTER ONE

*** * ***

THE CALL TO WAKEFULNESS

There comes a moment in every human life when something inside quietly whispers, "Wake up." For some, it is a soft stirring. For others, it is a sudden jolt—an inner quake that makes the life they've always lived feel strangely too small. And for many, it begins as an unnamed discomfort...a subtle ache that says, "There is more." More to God. More to yourself. More to life than the routine you inherited.

The Oxford definition of awakening speaks of "becoming suddenly aware of something." But spiritually, awakening is less like a lightning strike and more like a dimmer switch slowly turning up, revealing a room you've been sitting in all along. You don't wake up all at once. You wake up in layers. And even the layers have layers.

The Human Condition: Spirit Half-Asleep
Most of humanity lives in a kind of spiritual sleep; eyes open, heart dimmed, spirit distracted. Not because people are bad, but because the world trains us from birth to forget the most important thing: You are more than you were told. You were conditioned:
- to trust the outer world more than the inner
- to respond from fear rather than truth
- to chase approval rather than alignment
- to believe what others said instead of listening to the still, small Voice

This is why awakening feels more like remembering than learning. The truth hasn't been missing, you were simply looking everywhere but inward.

As Jesus said, "The kingdom of heaven is within you"—not above you, not far away, not reserved for the spiritual elite... *within you*. Awakening begins the moment you take that seriously.

The First Sign of Awakening: Dissatisfaction

Spiritual dissatisfaction is not a flaw—it is an invitation. Something in you starts feeling misaligned with:

- superficial answers
- empty explanations
- cultural noise
- inherited beliefs
- your own patterns
- the identity you were taught to carry

You start seeing cracks in the story you once accepted blindly. "If my spirit is restless, what is it trying to tell me?" The answer is already woven into the discomfort: your inner life is outgrowing your old life. Awakening is not a crisis. It is growth felt from the inside.

The Second Sign: The Search Begins

Once the ache begins, you start searching—even if you don't call it a search. You might find yourself asking: "Who am I really?", "Why am I here?", "Why does life feel both familiar and foreign?", "Why do I sense a truth I can't explain yet?"

These are not ordinary questions. They are symptoms of the inner eye starting to open. As Rumi wrote, "What you seek is seeking you."

You search because truth is calling. You feel the ache because truth is near. The search is not about collecting answers, it is about becoming the one who can receive them.

The Third Sign: The Light Remembers Itself

There comes a moment—sometimes fleeting, sometimes overwhelming, when something within you recognizes something greater than you:

- a moment of clarity
- a moment of peace
- a moment where time pauses long enough for you to feel the Presence beneath everything

This is not imagination. This is memory. The Light in you remembering Itself.

Even science nods in this direction: studies show that profound moments of awe shift the brain into patterns of coherence, the same patterns found in deep meditation and prayer. It seems the body recognizes truth before the mind finds words for it.

The World Will Not Congratulate You

Awakening rarely receives applause. People around you may not understand. Some will feel threatened. Some will think you're "changing." (Some even panic if you turn down plans to "be in silence," as if that's suspicious behavior). Your awakening will sometimes reveal who was connected to your spirit and who was only connected to your patterns.

"What if the misunderstanding of others is simply proof that I am becoming myself?" The answer: growth always reveals truth—both in you and around you.

The Cosmic Irony: You Wake Up to What Was Always There

The greatest surprise of awakening is discovering that nothing was ever missing. You were not cut off. You were not abandoned. You were not spiritually defective. You were simply asleep.

As Eckhart Tolle reminds us, "The moment you realize you are not present, you are present."

Awakening is remembering. Presence is returning. Truth is unveiling. Love is reclaiming. Light is recognizing itself in you.

Awakening Is the Beginning, Not the End

Do not expect your life to become instantly perfect. Do not expect all confusion to disappear. Do not expect the ego to cheer joyfully as you outgrow it. If anything, your ego will file a strongly worded complaint.

Transformation is underway, yes; but it is only beginning. Awakening is not the summit. It is the first step out of the valley. The mountain is ahead. And the Light that called you, will guide you.

The Call to Wakefulness

There is a reason this chapter is first. Nothing else in this book will matter if you have not recognized the call within yourself. Here is the truth. If you are reading these words:

- you have already begun waking up
- you would not hunger for Light if Light were not stirring inside you
- you would not notice the ache if your spirit were not expanding
- you would not question the world if you were not starting to see beyond it

Awakening is not something you accomplish. It is something you allow. It is the soul hearing God whisper, "Rise." And responding, "I'm listening."

When the soul says, "Wake up," it isn't condemning you, it's inviting you. Inviting you out of survival mode and into Presence. Out of inherited perception and into truth. Because awakening changes the way you see everything: God, yourself, other people, and even your ordinary day. Chapter 2 is about that shift; seeing with new eyes.

* * *

Key Insight

Awakening is not the discovery of something new, but the remembrance of something eternal. It begins the moment you see that the life you've been living is too small for the truth you carry.

Reflection Practice

When did I first sense the subtle ache that "there is more"?
What beliefs or assumptions am I outgrowing? What is awakening whispering to me right now?
Am I willing to follow the call, even if I don't see the whole path?

Wakefulness begins when you stop ignoring the quiet call within you. Next, we'll explore how awakening changes what you can see—learning to see with new eyes.

CHAPTER TWO

* * *

SEEING WITH NEW EYES

Awakening always begins with sight—but not with the eyes in your head. It begins when the inner eye starts to open, even if only a little, and you suddenly sense that what you called "the world"... was only the surface of it.

Most people move through life assuming the visible world is the whole world. But if the visible world were the whole world, why would your deepest clarity so often come when your physical eyes are closed?

"The real act of discovery consists not in seeking new landscapes, but in having new eyes."—Marcel Proust

New eyes do not mean different scenery. They mean different seeing, a shift in the one who is looking. And when your perception shifts, your experience of reality shifts with it.

This isn't just spiritual poetry. Even modern physics quietly agrees: in the quantum realm, particles behave differently when they are observed. It is as if *how* you look changes what you are looking at.

If matter itself responds to being seen, what might your life do when you begin to see differently?

The Holographic Nature of Reality

Most people think of life as a straight line; one event after another, like beads on a string. You are born, you grow up, you go to school, you work, you retire. Birth ~ life ~ death.

Simple. Flat. Linear.

But once your inner sight begins to awaken, the line starts to bend. You notice strange repetitions and patterns. Moments that mirror other moments. Lessons that seem to come back wearing new clothes. You begin noticing:

- recurring themes
- repeated emotional patterns
- similar kinds of people showing up
- symbolic "coincidences"
- the same lesson appearing in different situations
- a kind of personal "echo" in your circumstances

Life starts to feel less like a straight line and more like a living tapestry, threads weaving in and out of one another. This is what I mean when I say life is holographic: each part contains something of the whole, and the whole expresses itself through every part. Jesus said, "If your eye is single, your whole body will be full of light." A "single" eye is not a physical condition...it is a unified way of seeing. It sees:

- pattern instead of randomness
- meaning instead of emptiness
- unity instead of fragmentation

"If everything in my life were symbolic, what might it be saying?" The answer is hidden inside the question itself: life is always speaking, but you hear it according to how you see it.

Truth Has No Conflict With Itself

Truth is never at war. Only perception is. The Light never argues with the darkness. It doesn't need to. It simply shines, and the argument ends. Yet when you look at the world, it appears full of conflict:

- religion against religion
- idea against idea
- "my truth" against "your truth"

We confuse our ideas about truth with truth itself. Truth doesn't fracture. Our beliefs about it do. Our interpretations do. Our fears do. This is why the inner life can feel so divided. Not because the truth is split, but because we are. When your sight begins to heal:

- you start seeing where you were arguing with reality
- you notice where your beliefs were smaller than the truth
- you recognize that many of your "contradictions" lived only in the mind

The Light has no problem with itself. It is our divided seeing that creates tension. New eyes do not necessarily give you new doctrines, but they heal the conflict in how you hold them.

Stillness Clears the Lens

You do not see with new eyes by trying harder. You see with new eyes when you become still enough to let reality show itself to you. Stillness doesn't manufacture truth...it reveals it. But the mind will fight stillness with everything it has. It says things like:

- "You're too distracted."
- "This is a waste of time."
- "You're not 'good' at meditation."
- "Nothing is happening."
- "You should be doing something productive."

Notice how every one of those thoughts assumes the same thing: that stillness is about performance. It is not. Stillness is not the absence of thought—it is the growing awareness that you are not your thoughts. Thoughts can come and go. They always have, and they always will. But you are the one who sees them.

Even neuroscience points in this direction. Studies show that when we rest in focused, gentle awareness:

- the brain shifts into more coherent rhythms
- stress responses quiet down
- the "fight or flight" system relaxes
- clarity and creativity increase

Stillness wipes the lens of perception clean. It doesn't change the Light. It simply removes what was blocking it.

Humor Helps You See Differently

Spiritual sight does not require spiritual seriousness. Some people approach awakening with the same intensity as cramming for a final exam, brows furrowed, shoulders tense, soul holding its breath. But insight often arrives in the very moment you exhale, in a smile, a laugh, or an unexpected sense of lightness.

Humor is a small kind of surrender. You momentarily stop taking your mind's drama so seriously, and in that crack, Light can slip through. G.K. Chesterton once wrote, "Angels can fly because they can take themselves lightly."

Sometimes, the most spiritual thing you can do is to laugh at your own ego kindly. Not in mockery, but in relief.

Living With New Eyes

Seeing with new eyes is not about escaping the world. It is about seeing the same world differently:

- the same job, but a different relationship with it
- the same family, but a deeper compassion for them
- the same challenges, but a clearer sense of what they are shaping in you
- the same body, but a growing reverence for the life within it

You may still live in the same town, in the same house, driving the same car, drinking the same coffee. But something in you has shifted. The axis of awareness has moved. Reality becomes more than an arrangement of objects; it becomes a conversation. You are no longer just in life. Life is also in you. You wake up in the morning not simply into another long day, but into an ongoing dialogue with God, with truth, with the universe and Light that surrounds you and is within you.

The external world may look unchanged. But what you see in it, what you sense through it, and what you receive from it will never be the same.

New eyes don't give you a new world; they reveal the world that was always there. And once you can see clearly, the next step is alignment: letting vision become living.

Today, pause once and ask, *"What is the truest response here?"*

* * *

Key Insight

Seeing with new eyes means recognizing that life is not random, but symbolic and connected...a living conversation between you, God, and the field of reality. The Light has never been absent. New eyes simply let you finally notice it.

Reflection Practice

Where in my life do I keep seeing the same pattern or lesson?

What situation might be inviting me to see deeper than the surface?

What happens when I pause, become still, and ask, "What is this moment trying to show me?"

How might a little humor soften my perspective on something that feels heavy right now?

CHAPTER THREE

* * *

ALIGNMENT: WHEN SEEING BECOMES LIVING

Seeing is the first miracle. Alignment is the second. Awakening begins when you start to see differently. Alignment begins when you start to live differently. Not because someone told you to. Not because you're trying to be "better." But because the truth you've seen will not let you live the way you used to.

Alignment is what happens when your inner sight and your outer life begin to walk in the same direction. It is when: the mind bows to the heart, the heart bows to the Spirit, and the false bows to the Real. You do not align by force. You align by agreement.

Jesus said, "My sheep hear My voice." Sometimes that voice is a clear word. Sometimes it's a nudge. Sometimes it's the quiet sense that you can't keep living out of sync with what you now know in your soul.

What Alignment Feels Like
Alignment is not a state of perfection. It is a state of coherence. Coherence feels like:

- "I'm not fighting myself as much."
- "I don't betray my own knowing as easily."
- "I can feel when something is off inside, even if I can't name it yet." When you are aligned:
- decisions feel cleaner
- your "no" becomes honest,
- your "yes" becomes real
- you recover from triggers more quickly
- you notice when you're slipping and gently return instead of spiraling

Alignment is not about becoming flawless. It is about becoming true.

Signs You Are Moving Into Alignment

You Pause Before Reacting: You find yourself taking a breath in places you used to explode. You don't always get it "right," but now you notice the gap between the stimulus and your response. That small gap is where alignment lives.

"Why does this situation feel different now, even though nothing outside changed?" The answer... you changed.

You Feel "Off" When You Step Out of Truth: You can no longer say certain things, agree to certain things, or participate in certain dynamics without feeling a quiet dissonance inside. Your spirit grieves where it used to be numb.

That discomfort is not condemnation, it is alignment trying to pull you back to yourself.

Peace Shows Up in Strange Places: Places that used to trigger you; traffic, delays, criticism, uncertainty, don't own you like they used to. You may still feel irritation, but it doesn't hijack your entire inner world. Peace appears in the middle of situations where it "shouldn't" make sense.

Your Intuition Starts Speaking Up: You begin hearing the subtle "yes" and "no" more clearly. You might not always like what it says. But you trust it more. And life goes better when you listen.

You Become Harder to Manipulate: Not because you're suspicious, but because you're clear. Confusion is fertile soil for manipulation. Clarity is not. A person aligned with truth becomes very difficult to control with guilt, fear, or flattery.

The Quiet Science of Alignment

Modern research on heart–brain coherence shows that when people shift into emotions like appreciation, gratitude, or compassion, the patterns of their heartbeat and brain waves become smooth and synchronized. In that state:

- thinking clears
- reactions calm

- creativity rises
- stress responses ease

In other words, when love and truth are centered in your awareness, your nervous system literally becomes more ordered.

What spiritual wisdom has always called "peace" is being measured as coherence. Alignment is not just a spiritual idea. It is something your entire being recognizes.

Why We Drift

You don't usually fall out of alignment in one dramatic moment. You drift. You drift when:

- you bite your tongue instead of speaking the truth
- you're called to speak
- you say "yes" to what you know is "no" inside
- you rehearse fear instead of practicing trust
- you ignore what your heart has already shown you

It rarely begins with a huge betrayal. It often starts with something small:

- "I'll deal with this later."
- "This isn't a big deal."
- "I'll stay where it's comfortable just a little longer."

But even when you drift, something in you knows. And the moment you admit, "I'm out of alignment," you are already turning back toward it. Awareness is always the first step home.

Misalignment Is Feedback, Not Failure

Most of us were trained to see every misstep as moral failure. But spiritually, misalignment is more like a dashboard warning light. It doesn't mean the car is ruined. It means something needs attention.

Your spirit never weaponizes your mistakes against you. The ego does that. Shame does that. Your spirit simply says: "You're not being who you are. Come back." It is not angry at you. It is standing at the door of your awareness, patiently knocking.

Alignment and Love

Alignment is not just about making "right choices." It is about letting love become the true center of your being. When you are aligned with love:

- you don't have to force patience—it arises
- kindness feels natural, not like a performance
- forgiveness becomes *possible* where it once felt *impossible*
- boundaries become clear, not harsh
- mercy and wisdom begin to move together

When Jesus said, "Love your neighbor as yourself," He wasn't merely proposing a moral challenge...He was describing an alignment of being. You cannot fully love others if you are at war within yourself.

As you align with the truth of who God says you are, love flows more freely in every direction.

The Deepest Evidence of Alignment

The deepest evidence is not that you; never get triggered, always know what to do, or float through life peacefully like a cloud. The deepest evidence is that:

- your presence changes,
- people feel calmer around you,
- conversations deepen naturally
- others feel seen, not judged
- you carry an atmosphere of "it's okay to be real here"

This is what it means to be "salt" and "light" in the world: not loud, not pushy, not showy—simply present, simply aligned. You become a mirror where others can glimpse their own Light.

Alignment Is a Returning, Not a Destination

You will not reach a day where you say, "I am now fully aligned forever." Life is not static. Situations change. Layers surface. Old patterns sometimes revisit to see if you still believe them.

Alignment is not a trophy. It is a rhythm. You fall out of sync -> you notice -> you return...again and again. But each time, you come back a little faster, a little gentler, a little wiser. You are not starting from scratch each time. You are spiraling deeper into truth.

One Breath Away

The most hopeful thing about alignment is this: You are never as far from it as you think. You are one honest breath away. One moment of saying, "I'm off, and that's okay, but I want to return." One quiet turning of your attention toward the Light within you.

Alignment is not about earning God's nearness. It is about remembering it. God has not stepped away from you. You have simply stepped away from yourself. The journey back is always shorter than the story you tell about it.

Alignment is what happens when truth stops being information and becomes direction. Next we move into embodiment; when truth becomes identity.

May what you've seen begin to settle into your bones...gently, steadily, and fully.

* * *

Key Insight

Alignment is not spiritual perfection; it is inner coherence. It is the ongoing choice to let what you know in your deepest place shape how you live in your everyday life.

Reflection Practice

Where in my life do I feel "off," even if I can't explain why yet?

When have I recently acted against what I knew was true in my heart?

What would one small act of alignment look like for me today?

How might my presence change if I allowed love, not fear, to be my true center?

CHAPTER FOUR

* * *

EMBODIMENT: TRUTH BECOMING IDENTITY

We are meant to live every moment with a growth mindset. When something ceases to grow, it stagnates, and stagnation is the opposite of spiritual life.

As I look back over my own journey, I can see blessings and challenges woven together, as they are for all of us. But the past six years have been different. They have been marked by a quiet, persistent guidance I didn't even realize I needed—almost as if awakening had been growing in me long before I ever called it by name.

Living in the present moment, the Now, opens a continual awareness of the beauty and wholeness life has been offering all along. Peace and joy are not fragile visitors, they are steady residents whose light is only dimmed by distraction. And let me be clear: I do not have everything "figured out." I do not claim to have special knowledge or a superior path. We are all equal in the eyes of our Creator.

Paul reminded us of this when he wrote that there is always more to know than what you know. He wasn't discouraging certainty—he was inviting openness, as if to say, "Relax. You don't have to know everything to walk in what you do know."

Embodiment is not the result of exhaustive understanding; it is the fruit of willingness, presence, and surrender. You grow because you are alive, not because you have mastered every secret of the universe. This is what allows embodiment to be joyful instead of heavy...a journey of continual becoming, not a test you must pass.

Living in the present moment makes you more whole; not occasionally, not accidentally, but naturally–quietly–steadily.

In presence, you begin to live as the "lesser yet beautiful light of The Light." God living through you. Life expressing through you. Truth becoming you. And this is where embodiment begins.

The Key to Living Is Being

The spiritual path is not about trying harder. It's about becoming softer. Not performing more, but being more. The key to living is Being: allowing your thoughts, words, and actions to arise from unconditional love. When love becomes the motivation behind what you do, you are no longer "trying to be spiritual." You are simply letting truth express itself.

Woven into the fabric of the universe is a simple principle: What you give in purity returns multiplied. This is not mere karma, as some call it. This is coherence...truth returning to greet itself in you. When you live from Being:

- you begin to see light in all circumstances
- joy arises not just in blessings, but in challenges
- peace becomes your default instead of your exception
- clarity replaces confusion
- your choices become aligned instead of reactive

"If God already completed the work, what is left but to live it?"
The answer is hidden in the question: embodiment is the living of what God already finished.

Balance: The Atmosphere of Embodiment

To remain in the flow of peace, balance becomes essential. Balance in:

- mind
- emotion
- body
- spirit
- rest and action
- solitude and connection
- giving and receiving

Balance is not something you achieve once, it is something you return to repeatedly. It is the "center" from which embodiment breathes. And one of the most practical tools for restoring balance is breath. When the world overwhelms you, when your emotions shake, when your mind races, when uncertainty rises...your breath is the doorway home.

Spiritual teachers have always known this. Science is only now catching up. A field of research called heart-brain coherence shows that focused breathing reorganizes the nervous system into clarity.

Focused breathing brings balance. When you're overwhelmed or injured, someone will say, "Just breathe." It's practical advice: steady breathing can shift you out of fight-or-flight, reduce physiological stress, and restore clearer thinking. Your inner world becomes harmonious again. Your body comes back into alignment with truth. Breath is the simplest form of embodiment.

It's easy to forget how much of life depends on realities we cannot see. You trust the invisible frequencies that carry images and sound, the unseen signals that guide planes, the quiet currents that connect the world. In the same way, breath becomes a simple way of tuning your inner life, returning you to balance when you feel pulled off-center.

Stillness Is Not Impossible

The mind often lies and says:
- "Stillness is too hard."
- "Your thoughts are too loud."
- "You're not spiritual enough."
- "Other people can meditate—you can't."
- "You're just too busy."

These are not truths. They are symptoms of inner noise. Stillness is not the absence of thought, it is the recognition that you are not your thoughts.

Quieting the mind depends less on skill and more on willingness and belief. Stillness is not reserved for monks. Stillness is your birthright. Even a few seconds of real presence creates more transformation than hours of anxious thinking.

"If stillness is my natural state, why doubt my ability to return to it?"

Stillness is simply remembering.

The Power of Visualization

Visualization is often misunderstood. It is not about "wishing." It is about aligning perception with truth. Visualization is the mind cooperating with Spirit, the heart painting the inner picture of what your soul already knows.

When you visualize from a place of peace, you are not imagining something into existence. You are remembering something that is already true in the deeper realm. This is why Jesus said, "Believe that you have received it, and it will be yours."

Not "believe that you might receive it." Believe you have, because in the realm of Spirit, it is already finished. Visualization is not asking God to do more—it is letting yourself see what God already did.

Living From Love

When unconditional love becomes the motivation behind your Being:
- patience flows,
- compassion deepens,
- generosity expands,
- presence stabilizes,
- grace becomes effortless
- joy becomes natural
- clarity becomes grounded
- fear loses its grip

Love is not something you try to manufacture...it is what arises when you stop resisting who you are. You are an expression of the Source, a flame of the Greater Flame, a voice of the Word, a wave of the Infinite Sea. Embodiment is simply the recognition of this truth, and the willingness to live from it.

Identity Rooted in the Light

The world suffers from an identity crisis. Many of us identify with the self that wants to im-press others—the false self—rather than the true self that longs to ex-press love. But your deepest identity is not something you manufacture; it is something you receive. In the words of the psalmist, you are "beautifully and wonderfully made."

And here is the doorway into that true identity: accept the Grace that awaits. Not as a "one and done" moment, but as a constant, continual embracing of it. Grace is offered to everyone, but it transforms only those who receive it.

The more you embrace Being, the more your identity shifts from:
- doing to being
- fear to freedom
- confusion to clarity
- effort to flow
- performance to presence

Embodiment is not about spiritual achievement. It is about letting truth animate your life from the inside out. You do not transform into anything new, you reveal what has always been there. You are becoming who you already are.

Truth embodied is no longer a belief you visit...it becomes the place you live from. And what tries to leave you will often resist on the way out; this is where transformation begins to burn.

What in you is asking to be refined, not punished, but made free?

* * *

Key Insight
Embodiment is the shift from knowing truth to being the expression of truth. It is not earned through mastery, but revealed through presence, balance, and love. You grow because you are alive—not because you understand everything.

Reflection Practice
Where today did I act from Being rather than habit?

What truth is ready to be lived instead of simply understood?

What would change if every choice today were motivated by unconditional love?

Which part of me needs breath and balance right now?

PART II — HEALING THE INNER LANDSCAPE

Awakening opens your eyes. But healing is what helps you live what you've seen. Part II is where the work becomes intimate—not heavy, not condemning, but honest. Because once you begin to wake up, you also begin to notice what has been shaping you from beneath the surface: old fears, protective patterns, false identities, and the inner splits we learned simply to survive.

Most of us were never taught how to live whole.

We were taught:
- How to cope.
- How to perform.
- How to manage pain without touching it.
- Healing is different.

Healing doesn't mean you "fix yourself" through pressure or perfection. It means you stop abandoning yourself. You bring what is hidden into the Light—without shame—and allow truth to do what truth does: restore, integrate, and make you free.

In this section we move through the flames of transformation, the healing of inner division, and the end of fear—not by force, but by clarity. You'll begin learning how fear works, why it repeats, and how it loses power when it is seen. You'll also begin practicing a new relationship to your inner world: not reacting to every thought, not believing every story, and not living from old wounds as if they are your identity.

This is the inner landscape—where your deepest habits were formed, and where your deepest freedom begins.

You don't heal by becoming someone else. You heal by returning to who you truly are.

What part of you has been asking—quietly—for safety, truth, and wholeness?

CHAPTER FIVE

* * *

THE FLAMES OF TRANSFORMATION

There are seasons when awakening feels gentle; like dawn slowly brightening the edges of your world. And there are seasons when it feels like fire. Not the fire of punishment, but the fire of transformation.

The ancients spoke of God as a "consuming fire," not because divine love delights in destroying, but because Love is too real to coexist forever with illusion. What cannot endure in that fire is never your true self. It is everything you are not—every lie, every false identity, every fear masquerading as truth.

On the edge of a small town, there was a refiner who worked late into the night.

People said his workshop was too quiet, too dim, too simple to be the place where anything important happened. But if you stepped inside, you would see a small furnace glowing with steady light, and beside it a man with a calm, watchful gaze.

One evening, a young apprentice came to him, carrying a lump of dull, rough metal in both hands.

"Everyone tells me there's gold in here," the apprentice said, "but I don't see it. I've tried polishing the outside. I've tried chipping away the ugly parts. I've even tried hiding it so no one will notice how ordinary it looks. Nothing works. If there is anything precious in this, I can't find it."

The refiner did not argue. He simply took the metal, weighed it carefully in his hand, and placed it inside the fire.

Almost immediately, the apprentice grew anxious.

"Is that necessary?" he asked. "Can't you just clean it? Or bless it? Or...do something less painful?"

The refiner's eyes stayed on the flame.

"If this metal could speak," he answered quietly, "it would say the same thing. It does not understand the fire. It only feels the heat. But I am not here to destroy what is precious. I am here to reveal it."

As the temperature rose, the metal began to change—slowly at first, then more visibly. What had seemed solid and unmoving started to soften. Dark streaks within it loosened and rose to the surface.

The apprentice stepped back, alarmed.

"It's falling apart," he said. "You're ruining it."

The refiner gently skimmed away the dark film that had surfaced, never taking his eyes off the glowing metal.

"This is not its ruin," he said. "This is its revealing. The fire does not create the gold. It uncovers it."

"How do you know when it's ready?" the apprentice asked. The refiner smiled, still watching.

"When I can see my own reflection in it," he replied, "I know the fire has done its work."

The apprentice fell silent.

At that moment, he realized something: his life was the metal, and he was standing in the doorway of his own refining. Part of him wanted to run. Part of him wanted to trust.

Both were real. Only one would lead him into who he truly was.
He took a breath, stepped a little closer to the light, and whispered, almost too softly to hear:

"Do in me what you're doing to that gold...even if I don't understand it yet." The refiner nodded, as if he had been waiting for those words all along.

Many people hope for spiritual awakening without the flames. They want light without heat, insight without disruption, growth without discomfort.

But to awaken is to be willing to step into a fire that burns away what no longer belongs to you.

When Truth Becomes Fire

Truth can arrive softly; like a quiet inner knowing. But there comes a point when truth stops being just an idea you admire and becomes a fire you cannot escape.

- A relationship you know is rooted in fear instead of love.
- A habit that keeps you numb instead of present.
- A belief about God that no longer fits what your spirit knows to be true.
- A way of living that looks "successful" on the outside but is slowly hollowing you out inside.

For a while:

- You can ignore it.
- You can excuse it.
- You can spiritualize it.
- You can say, "It's not that bad," or "Maybe later," or "This is just how life is."

But when the inner light grows stronger, truth begins to press in. What you could tolerate before you now feel more clearly. What you once justified now starts to disturb you. The "peace" you had was not peace at all—it was just successful distraction. This pressure is not God turning against you. It is Love turning up the flame.

The Spirit does not expose what is false to shame you, but to free you. Yet the ego interprets this exposure as judgment. It says, "If I let this go, I will lose myself." The truth is the opposite: if you don't let it go, you will keep losing yourself.

The flames of transformation are simply truth and love at full intensity.

The Refiner's Fire

Scripture uses the image of a refiner's fire; metal heated until impurities rise to the surface and can be removed. The goal is not to destroy the gold, but to reveal it.

Just as the earlier parable points towards, think of your soul as that gold. Within you is a core of uncreated light, an image of God that cannot be erased. Around that core, throughout your life, layers have formed: fear, shame, defensiveness, people-pleasing, self-hatred, unforgiveness, pride, and endless attempts to prove your worth.

If you only ever ask for comfort, you may never see how thick those layers have become.

But when your heart cries out for more—more reality, more freedom, more of God—something begins to happen. That cry is heard. Grace responds. The temperature rises. Old patterns stop working. Old illusions are disturbed. Old hiding places no longer feel safe.

This can be frightening if you think God's goal is to punish or humiliate you. But the Refiner's attention is not on the dross; it is on the gold. He never takes His eyes off what is precious.

The heat is not against you; it is for you.

Intense Desire: The Inner Flame

Many spiritual teachers, across cultures and centuries, have said in different words a similar thing: true transformation requires intense desire; not casual interest, not vague curiosity—a deep, focused, burning yes.

This intense desire is not about earning grace. You are not trying to twist God's arm. You are allowing your whole being to align with what Grace already wants to give.

When your desire for truth becomes singular—when you want reality more than you want to be right, more than you want to stay comfortable—that desire itself becomes a flame. It is the fire of longing that draws you into the fire of God.

This is what some have called singleness of purpose: a heart that is no longer trying to serve two masters; Truth and appearance, Love and fear, Spirit and ego. It doesn't mean you never struggle again. It means that beneath every struggle, your deepest yes belongs to God.

This intensity is what burns away half-heartedness, lukewarm living, and spiritual complacency. It is the difference between reading about the fire and actually stepping into it.

What the Fire Burns Away

The flames of transformation do not attack your humanity. They expose and consume what hinders your humanity from reflecting its true Source. What do these flames burn away?

- **False identities** – the roles you cling to as a substitute for your true self: "the successful one," "the needed one," "the victim," "the strong one who never needs help."
- **Attachment to outcome** – the belief that your worth depends on life unfolding according to your script.
- **Hidden agreements with fear** – the quiet ways you say, "I'll obey as long as I stay safe," or "I'll trust as long as I stay in control."
- **Resentments and judgments** – the stories you rehearse that keep an old wound alive, long after the event has passed.
- **Beliefs about God that are too small** – pictures of a distant, punitive deity that keep you from resting in the truth of Love.

As these begin to surface, the ego panics: "If I let go of this, who will I be?" The answer is simple...you will be more yourself than you have ever been. The fire does not erase you. It reveals you.

What the Fire Awakens

As the flames of transformation do their work, something else emerges, quietly but unmistakably:

- **A deeper honesty with yourself.** You stop pretending you are fine when you are not. You stop manipulating appearances for approval. You tell the truth, first to God, then to yourself, then to others.
- **A growing tenderness toward others.** You realize how much you've been forgiven, how patient Love has been with you.

You become slower to condemn, quicker to understand, more willing to see the light buried under someone else's confusion.

- **A more grounded freedom.** You still feel fear, but it no longer has the final vote. You become willing to take steps you once avoided, to risk obedience in ways that once seemed impossible.
- **A deeper trust.** Even in uncertainty, there is an inner knowing: "I am held. I am not being punished; I am being purified. I may not understand the details, but I trust the heart of the One who holds the fire."

The flames do not just take things away; they give you a clearer, simpler, truer way of being.

Transformation and Suffering

It would be dishonest to speak of the flames of transformation and ignore the role of suffering. Not all suffering is transformative by itself. Pain alone does not automatically awaken. Many people are wounded and become only more bitter, cynical, and closed off.

Suffering becomes transformative when it is held in truth and grace.

When you bring your pain into the Presence—when, instead of only asking, "Why is this happening to me?" you also ask, "How can this be used? What is being revealed? What is being healed?"—then even the darkest season can become part of the refining.

This does not mean God wills every wound, every injustice, every loss. It does mean that nothing is beyond His ability to weave into redemption. The cross and resurrection are the pattern written into the fabric of reality: loss and rising, death and new life, surrender and unexpected joy.

To follow Christ is not to bypass this pattern, but to walk it with Him. When you offer your pain into the flames, you are not glorifying suffering as an end in itself. You are allowing what was meant for evil to be folded into a deeper good you cannot yet see.

Cooperation, Not Perfectionism

Hearing that transformation involves effort and intense desire can stir old religious wounds. Many were taught a harsh perfectionism:

"If you were really spiritual, you wouldn't struggle. If you had enough faith, you would never doubt, never fear, never falter." That is not the truth. You are not being invited into spiritual performance. You are being invited into cooperation.

You cannot kindle the fire on your own. You cannot manufacture grace. But you can:

- Bring dry wood instead of soaked excuses.
- Open windows instead of sealing every crack.
- Stop pouring water on the flame with cynicism and self-sabotage.

In other words, you can stop resisting what Love is already trying to do. Transformation is not about proving yourself to God. It is about letting God prove His love in you.

All the promises of God are "yes" in Christ. Your part is the "so be it"—the amen of your life. The flames of transformation are what happen when His yes and your yes meet.

How to Step Into the Flames

What does stepping into the flames of transformation actually look like in daily life? It is often surprisingly simple—and surprisingly costly.

Tell the truth, no matter how small. Begin with honest prayer: "God, here is what I really feel. Here is what I really fear. Here is what I'm still clinging to." Truth spoken in the presence of Love is fire.

- **Bring your patterns into the light.** Notice where you keep circling the same mountain, same argument, same temptation, same self-sabotage. Instead of hiding it, ask: "What is this pattern protecting? What lie is underneath it?" Offer that lie into the flames.
- **Say a deeper yes.** Choose one area where you have been half-hearted. Maybe it's a habit you know is numbing you, a calling you've ignored, a conversation you've avoided, a step of obedience you've postponed. Ask for courage and take one concrete step.

- **Stay when everything in you wants to run.** Fire is uncomfortable. When conviction arises, you will feel the urge to distract yourself—scroll, binge, overwork, overtalk, overspiritualize. Instead of running, stay present. Breathe. Ask, "What are You showing me?" and listen.
- **Trust that what remains is real.** As certain roles, relationships, or illusions fall away, grief is natural. But remember: whatever cannot survive the fire was never your foundation. What remains after the flames is more solid than what you lost.

You Are Safe in the Fire

The greatest fear is often this: "If I let God all the way in, will anything be left of me?" The answer from the heart of Love is: yes, only the *real* you.

The flames of transformation are not wild, uncontrolled destruction. They are the focused fire of a Love that knows exactly what it is doing. Not a hair of your true self is singed. You are not called to manage the temperature of the fire. You are called to trust the One who tends it.

In time, you may look back on the very seasons you begged God to remove and whisper, "Thank You." Not because the pain was good, but because something holy came out of it...something that could not have been formed any other way.

Your heart becomes humbler, clearer, more luminous. The light within you is less obstructed. You begin to live more honestly, more freely, more like the One in whose image you were made. The flames did not destroy you. They revealed the gold that had always been there.

The fire of God is not destruction; it is purification. And one of its first works is to heal the inner divide: the places you've learned to live in pieces.

Name one inner conflict you feel often, and simply tell the truth about it, without fixing it yet.

The fire of God is not destruction—it is purification. Next, we'll let that purifying light heal the inner divide—the places you've learned to live in pieces.

* * *

Key Insight

The flames of transformation are not punishment; they are love in motion. They burn away what is false, fearful, and borrowed, so that what is true, free, and God-born in you can shine without obstruction. Transformation is grace meeting your deepest yes—the refiner's fire revealing the gold that was there all along.

Reflection Practice

Name the fire you're in. Take a moment to honestly name one area of your life that feels like a fire right now. *Is it a relationship, a health struggle, a financial pressure, an inner conflict, a spiritual crisis?* Write it down without editing. Then gently ask: *"How might this be part of my refining, rather than proof of my rejection?"* You don't need a full answer. Just open to the possibility.

Identify what is being burned away. Ask yourself: *"In this situation, what is God inviting me to release?"* It might be control ... a grudge ... a false identity ... a belief that you are alone ... a picture of God as distant or cruel. Write it down. Imagine placing it into the fire, even if your emotions are not fully ready. Pray simply: "Burn away what is not true, and strengthen what is."

Pray for a deeper yes. Sit quietly and place your hand over your heart. Whisper: "I want what is real, even if it costs me what is not. Give me the courage to stay in the fire until only love remains." Stay in silence for a few breaths. Let this desire, even if small, be your flame.

CHAPTER SIX

* * *

HEALING THE SPLIT WITHIN

There is a kind of suffering deeper than any outward circumstance. It's the ache of being divided inside yourself. You feel it when you know one thing in your spirit but live another in your habits. When you tell others that God is love but secretly suspect you're the exception. When you've tasted moments of deep peace, yet still walk around with a low-grade inner tension you can't quite name.

It's the pain of being pulled in two directions at once; toward truth and toward illusion, toward love and toward fear, toward freedom and toward familiar bondage.

The apostle Paul once described this tension in words many people, religious or not, can recognize:

> "I don't do the good I want to do, but I keep on doing what I don't want to do." (paraphrased from Romans 7)

He wasn't describing a villain. He was describing a divided heart. Awakening makes this split more obvious. The flames of transformation (Chapter 5) expose it. But the goal is not to shame you with your dividedness. The goal is healing.

The Many Faces of the Inner Split

The split within rarely shows up with a label saying, "Hello, I am inner fragmentation." It disguises itself as normal life. It looks like:

- **Head vs. heart:** You *know* (intellectually) that you're loved, but deep down you still feel like you're on probation. You can explain grace, but you don't relax into it.

- **Sacred vs. "real life":** You have a "spiritual self" that shows up in prayer, at church, or during quiet moments, and a "regular self" doing emails, errands, dishes, and deadlines. They hardly ever talk.
- **Body vs. spirit:** Part of you believes the body is a problem, always suspect, always dragging your "higher" self-down. So you either indulge it and feel guilty, or ignore it and feel disconnected.
- **Public vs. private self:** The you that others see and the you lying awake at 2:00 a.m. feel like two different people—one curated, one raw.
- **Faith vs. fear:** You have real experiences of trust and real experiences of panic, and you bounce between them like a pendulum. On good days you're sure God's got you. On bad days you're pretty sure you've ruined everything beyond repair.

Underneath all of this lies one basic wound, the belief that you are fundamentally *two*, one self that is lovable and another self that is not. No wonder you're tired.

How the Split Is Born

No one comes into the world hating themselves or hiding from Love. The split is learned. It forms slowly through things like:

- **Conditioning and comparison:** From childhood, you're measured and labeled: good, bad, smart, slow, too emotional, too much, too quiet, too loud. You take notes. You learn which parts of you are rewarded and which are rejected. You start exiling pieces of your own heart just to belong.
- **Religious misunderstanding:** Many of us were told some version of, "God loves you... but also, you're basically disgusting to Him unless you fix it immediately." Instead of seeing sin, confusion, and wounding as illnesses to be healed, we start believing *we ourselves* are the disease.
- **Sacred/secular split:** You're taught that prayer, worship, and "ministry" are spiritual, while your job, parenting, grocery runs, and Netflix queue are "just life." Your soul starts living in two compartments that rarely meet; Sunday vs. Monday, devotion vs. dishes.

- **Unhealed wounds:** Betrayal, neglect, ridicule, abuse, or shame leave fractures inside. To cope, you build a "functional self" to survive out in the world while deeper parts of you hide in locked rooms, convinced they're not safe to bring into the light.

Over time, this fragmentation begins to feel normal. You might identify with your compensating patterns so strongly that you say, "That's just who I am." But your deepest self knows something's off. It remembers wholeness...even if it doesn't have language for it.

The Illusion of Two Selves

Within Christian language, we often hear about "old self" and "new self," "flesh" and "Spirit." If we misunderstand this, it can sound like there are two *equal* selves battling inside us; a "good me" who sincerely wants love and truth, and a "bad me" who is basically doomed and dragging everything down.

That's not the picture the deeper story is trying to paint.

Your true self is the you that God dreamed before any wound, lie, or label touched you... the real you, created in love, sustained in love, and destined to awaken fully in love. In the Christian story, this is the self "hidden with Christ in God," the "new creation."

Others might simply call this:

- your soul,
- your innermost being,
- your true nature,
- the light within.

Your false self is not another real nature. It's a *construction*; a collection of masks, fears, stories, defenses, personas, and survival strategies. It feels real because you've lived inside it. It has momentum, habits, and even some professional-grade excuses. But it doesn't have eternal substance.

The flames of transformation we explored in Chapter 5 are already aimed at *this* false self, not at your essence.

Love is not trying to burn the real you. Love is burning the split, the illusion that you are two.

Healing is not about eliminating your humanity. It's about letting Love untangle your true self from all the costumes you've had to wear.

Christ in You: The Center of Wholeness

If the problem is inner division, the solution is not the divided mind trying harder. If trying harder could have healed you, you'd be walking around as a glowing saint by now.

Wholeness is not something you manufacture by sheer willpower. Wholeness is a Presence you allow, a Life you awaken to.

The apostle Paul uses a breathtaking phrase for this: "Christ in you, the hope of glory." (Colossians 1:27) Not just Christ *for* you or Christ *beside* you, but Christ *in* you.

In the Christian story, this is the indwelling life of Jesus, the living center where all your scattered parts begin to come home.

If that language feels heavy because of your history with religion, you might hear it this way:

- the living Presence of God within,
- the Light at the core of your being,
- the divine spark,
- your true Self in God.

Different words, same mystery: there is a Love at the center of you that is wiser than your fear and more permanent than your wounds. From this Center:

- Your body is no longer the enemy; it becomes a temple, a partner in expressing love on earth.
- Your mind is not thrown away; it is renewed, gently untangled from lies and re-trained to see clearly.
- Your desires are not erased; they are purified, softened, and aimed toward what truly gives life.
- Your story is not discarded; it is re-read in the light of grace, with new meaning woven through old chapters.

The message of the gospel is not: *"Glue your shattered self together, behave better, and maybe God will think about accepting you."*

The message is closer to: *"You are already included in the life and love of God. Let your mind, heart, body, and story wake up to what is already true."*

You could say: In Christian language: Christ in you. In more universal language: the indwelling Presence of Love.

Different wording, same Light.

Healing the split within is really the process of letting every part of you; your thoughts, your emotions, your habits, your history, slowly come into agreement with that Presence.

It's less like fixing a broken machine and more like returning, again and again, to the One quiet Center inside you and letting it rearrange everything else.

Letting Go of War with Yourself

For many people, "spiritual life" has secretly become an inner civil war. They picture growth as a constant battle against themselves; suppressing desires, policing every thought, suspecting every emotion, and assuming that if there's any joy in it, it's probably not holy.

If spiritual life feels like boot camp with no graduation day, no wonder part of you wants to run.

Here's the problem: you cannot heal a split by increasing self-hatred. You cannot become whole by turning against your own heart. Love does not invite you to despise your humanity. Love invites you to offer it. What you bring into the light can be healed. What you keep in the dark stays frozen.

Healing begins when you dare to say: "Here is all of me... not just the polished parts I think You like, but the fear, anger, confusion, desire, fatigue, and doubt. I bring the *whole* of myself into Your presence."

That's not self-indulgence. That's surrender. The mask cannot be transformed. Only the real can.

The Body and the Spirit Reunited

One of the deepest fractures we carry is the split between body and spirit. Maybe you heard things like:

- "Your body just wants sin; your spirit wants God."
- "Spiritual people are above bodily needs."
- Or the classic: "Don't trust your feelings or your flesh."

The result? Your body becomes suspicious territory. You either indulge it and feel guilty, or ignore it and feel numb.

But in the Jesus story, the body is not an afterthought or an enemy:

- The Word becomes flesh.
- The Spirit fills bodies.
- Jesus is raised in a body.
- Paul calls the body a temple, not a trash can.

Your body is not the enemy of your spirit. *Your body is the instrument your spirit uses to express love here.*

Healing the split within includes mending this relationship:

- Listening to your limits instead of despising them.
- Letting your body participate in prayer...breath, posture, stillness, tears, laughter.
- Noticing where anxiety, shame, or fear live in your body, and inviting Love to meet you right there, not just in your thoughts.

When body and spirit stop fighting and start cooperating, spiritual life moves from something you think about on the couch to something you live with your whole being.

When Old Stories Still Echo

Even as healing begins, the old voices don't instantly evaporate. They'll say things like:

- "You haven't really changed. This is just a phase." "If people knew the real you, they'd leave."
- "God is probably disappointed...again."
- "What happened to you is proof you're unlovable."

These are the echoes of the false self, not the voice of God. The voice of Love doesn't flatter, but it also doesn't accuse. It invites. It clarifies. It tells the truth *and* stays.

One of the most important skills in healing the split is learning to recognize which inner voice you're agreeing with. Accusation divides you. Condemnation pins you to your worst moment. Shame says, "You *are* what happened to you."

Grace says, "This is not who you are. Let Me show you who you are in Me."

Again and again, the split heals as you gently shift your agreement, from the old echo to the deeper truth. You may have to do this a thousand times. That's okay. Healing is allowed to be repetitive.

How the Split Heals in Everyday Life

Healing the split within is not usually a cinematic moment with a soundtrack and slow motion. It's a series of small, honest movements toward integration. Very often, it looks like this:

Honest prayer instead of performance prayer: You stop praying the "ideal version" of yourself and start praying the *real* one.

- "I'm exhausted."
- "I'm angry with You."
- "I'm scared this will never change." You let your words catch up to your actual soul.

Inviting the Presence into ordinary moments: You begin to say simple things like, "Be with me in this," while doing the laundry, answering emails, or driving. You notice that the Presence doesn't just meet you in big prayers and big moments...it's already here. Even the mundane becomes a place where joy quietly appears.

Holding contradictions with compassion: Instead of shaming yourself for feeling two things at once; "Part of me trusts; part of me is terrified"; you admit both. You might pray, "Here's my yes and here's my fear. Meet me in the middle."

Letting sacred words read you, not just inform you: When you hear phrases like "new creation," "Christ in you," "hidden with Christ in God," or simply "beloved," you don't just file them away as religious ideas. You sit with them until they start challenging your inner self-rejection.

Receiving forgiveness as atmosphere, not emergency only: You stop treating grace as a rare medicine for huge failures and start seeing it as the air you breathe. You live in ongoing relationship, where returning is always possible and shame is never the final word.

You Are Not Two

Slowly, a new awareness takes root: "I am not two. I am one person, loved and held in God, learning to let all of me come into agreement with that Love."

Your mind, body, memories, emotions, desires, wounds, and gifts are not scattered enemies fighting for control. They are being gently gathered into a single, truer story.

You will still have conflicting thoughts. You will still have days where old patterns flare up. But the split is no longer your identity. Union is. You are not trying to create wholeness from scratch. You are waking up to a wholeness that has been holding you all along. As that realization deepens:

- You become less interested in pretending and more interested in being honest.
- You become less brutal with yourself and, ironically, more free to grow.
- You become less afraid of what might surface in the fire, because you trust the Refiner more than you fear the heat.
- You are no longer living as two different people. You are becoming who you truly are.

Much of our inner conflict comes from living divided, one part of us trying to be "acceptable," another part quietly longing to be true.

The false self works hard to manage perception, but the true self simply wants to be real. As healing begins, one of the first fruits is not perfection, but genuineness.

We are drawn to authenticity the way the lungs are drawn to air. We crave the real; the singer whose voice carries more than sound, whose honesty makes you feel what they feel; the actor so present that the story reaches past the screen and touches something in you. We recognize it instantly because our souls were made for it. And awareness is one of the surest ways it rises in us: when we are truly present, pretense falls away, the inner divide begins to close, and what remains is simple, clean, and real.

This is one way you can tell healing is happening: you feel less need to "impress," and more freedom to "express." You stop auditioning for love and start living from it. Not as a performance...as a presence.

Where in your life are you still performing...and what would change if you simply told the truth and stayed present?

Wholeness begins the moment you stop abandoning parts of yourself. And when the inner war quiets, fear loses its fuel.

May you feel the gentle strength of unity within, so fear has less and less to stand on.

* * *

Key Insight

The "split within" is not your true identity—it is a wound created by fear, shame, and misunderstanding. In the deepest truth, you are one whole person, held in the life and love of God. Healing is the process of letting every part of you come into agreement with that love, until your inner and outer life begin to tell the same story.

Reflection Practice

Name your splits. Take a few minutes and gently write:

"I believe ____but I live as if_____." "I tell others _____but secretly I think _____about myself."

Don't fix it yet. Just let it be seen on paper. Awareness is already healing.

Invite Love into one tension. Pick just *one* of those inner contradictions. Pray in your own words, or something like:

"Here is where I feel divided: _____. I invite Your Presence into this tension. Show me what is true. Heal what is wounded. Bring together what feels torn apart."

Sit in silence for a moment, even if it feels ordinary. The moment you invite it, healing has already begun.

Bless your own body. Place a hand over your heart, or your chest, or wherever you feel tension, and say slowly:

"Thank you for carrying me this far. I bless you. I ask Love to fill you. We're on the same team."

Notice any emotion or resistance that comes up. Offer *that* into the Presence too.

A simple daily prayer for wholeness. You might whisper this in the morning or before sleep:

"Spirit of Truth and Love, I am tired of being two. Show me who I am in You. Let my thoughts, desires, words, and actions come into harmony with Your love. Gather all of me into You. Make me whole, inside and out."

Mean what you can. Grace will meet even a shaky yes.

CHAPTER SEVEN

* * *

THE END OF FEAR

Fear rarely knocks first. It doesn't send a polite email saying, "Just to let you know, I'll be arriving next Thursday at 3:17 p.m." It just shows up...heart racing, thoughts spinning, imagination sprinting ten miles ahead of reality. Your fears rarely RSVP, but they always show up early. You know the feeling:

- A strange sensation in your body.
- No reply to a text.
- A bill you weren't expecting.
- A news headline.
- A silence from God that feels too long.

Before anything actually happens, your mind has already written the worst possible script, cast you in the starring role, and rehearsed the ending three times.

Fear is fast. Fear is loud. Fear feels true in the moment.

But what if most fear is not a prophecy, not a punishment, and not even a reliable guide. *What if fear is, more often than not, a story?*

Fear as Illusion (But Not Denial)

Let's be clear: there is a kind of fear that is healthy, that's not "illusion;" that's survival. The nervous system is doing its job. If you're standing at the edge of a cliff and you feel a jolt of caution, that's wisdom. We'll call that danger-awareness.

But much of what we call "fear" is not about immediate danger. It is about imagined futures and resurrected pasts:

- replaying what went wrong ten years ago,
- rehearsing what might go wrong tomorrow,

- building worst-case scenarios before we even get the test results,
- assuming silence means abandonment, and delay means disaster.

This kind of fear is not about what *is*; it's about what the mind has decided *might be*.

What is fear, except a story unexamined?

Fear takes a feeling in the body, adds a memory from the past, then sprinkles in a handful of "What if...?" and "Always..." and "Never..." and bakes it into a narrative:

"This always happens to me."

"Nothing ever works out."

"If I lose this, I will destroy everything."

"If people see the real me, they'll leave."

By the time the story is finished, your body is reacting to a movie that hasn't even been filmed.

This is what we mean by fear as *illusion*, not that nothing painful can ever happen, but that fear often presents itself as absolute truth when it is, in fact, a rough draft written by a frightened mind.

The flames of transformation are not only about burning away sin and false identities; they are also about burning away untrue stories, especially the ones fueled by fear.

Faith as Remembering

If fear is a story unexamined, then faith is not pretending you don't feel afraid. Faith is remembering what is more deeply true than the story fear is telling. Faith is not forcing yourself to feel confident. It is turning your attention back to the Reality that holds you.

In Christian language, it's: "We walk by faith, not by sight." (2 Corinthians 5:7)

That doesn't mean we ignore what is in front of us. It means we refuse to make our entire identity and future out of what our senses and anxious thoughts report in a single moment.

"Sight" here can be:

- the medical report,
- the bank account,
- the conflict,
- the silence,
- the feeling of emptiness,
- the echoes of old shame.

"Faith" is remembering:

- "Even here, I am not outside God."
- "Even now, Love has not abandoned me."
- "I am more than this moment, and this moment is not the whole story."

For some, that Reality is named in very specific terms: Christ in you, the Spirit, the Father's heart. Others might simply call it God, Source, the Presence, the field of Love. The vocabulary can vary; the movement is the same:

Fear says, "You are alone, at risk, and it's all on you."

Faith remembers, "I am held, I am loved, and I am not the only one working on this."

Faith does not always erase the feeling of fear, but it shifts authority: fear is no longer the final voice.

Walking by Faith, Not by Sight

So what does it *actually* look like to walk by faith in the middle of fear? It does not usually look like floating above your problems in a cloud of spiritual confidence. It looks much more ordinary:

- You feel fear in your body—and you name it instead of hiding it.
- You notice the catastrophic story your mind is writing—and you question it instead of marrying it.
- You remember the Presence within and around you—and you lean into it instead of spiraling alone.
- You take the next small, honest step you *can* see, even though you cannot see ten steps ahead.

Walking by faith is often as simple as moving with the light you have, instead of waiting to feel perfect peace before you move at all. You might pray:

"Here is what I fear. Here is the story I'm telling myself. Here is what I cannot control. I choose, even trembling, to trust that I am held in something larger than this moment. Show me the next step."

Fear demands a guaranteed outcome before it moves. Faith moves with relationship instead of guarantees. Faith says, "I may not know how this will work out, but I know the One who walks with me—and that is enough light for this step."

"Now We Know in Part..."

One of fear's favorite tricks is to pretend it is omniscient. Fear always speaks in absolutes:

- "This will never change."
- "You will always be this way."
- "This mistake has ruined everything."
- "Nothing good can come from this."

There is a strange comfort in these absolutes—they give the illusion of certainty, even if that certainty is miserable. Part of us would rather cling to a terrible "always" than stand in the open field of "I don't know yet."

But woven into Scripture is a freeing confession: "Now we know in part." (1 Corinthians 13:9)

We do not see the whole picture. We do not know the final outcome. We are not the author of the story.

For the ego, this is threatening. It prefers control, not mystery. For the awakening heart, this can become a doorway into peace.

If we know only "in part," then fear's absolute statements are always exaggerations. Faith does not require pretending you're fine. It invites you to say:

"From where I stand right now, this looks hopeless. But I admit that my perspective is partial. I will not make fear's version of the story the final word." You don't have to replace fear's story with a shiny, positive one. You only have to let go of the demand to know the ending, and trust that Love sees a wider horizon than you do.

Science & the Soul: Epigenetics and Fear Patterns

Fear isn't only spiritual and emotional; it's also biological. Your nervous system has been learning how to respond to life since the womb. Experiences of safety, love, chaos, neglect, and trauma all leave traces—not just in your memories, but in your body and even in your gene expression.

This is where epigenetics comes in. Very simply put, epigenetics looks at how our environment and experiences can switch certain genes "on" or "off" without changing the DNA code itself. It's like having a huge library of possible songs, and life experience influencing which tracks get played on repeat.

Fear patterns can be passed down through: family stories, behavior we witness growing up, and even, according to some research, through epigenetic marks shaped by the stress and trauma of previous generations.

If you grew up in a home where the world was constantly presented as unsafe, where anger exploded without warning, or where love felt inconsistent, your nervous system learned, "Be on guard. Expect the worst. Stay small. Stay hyper-aware."

The point is not to blame your biology or your ancestors, but to recognize: if fear feels automatic, it might be because, on some level, it *is*.

The good news? Epigenetics also tells us that healing experiences matter. New patterns of safety, trust, honesty, and love can begin to reshape which "tracks" get played most often.

Practices like:

- genuine connection and attachment,
- trauma-informed therapy,
- contemplative prayer and meditation,
- breathing and grounding exercises,
- honest community,

- and repeated experiences of grace when you expected rejection,

All of these send new signals into your system. You are not doomed to replay fear simply because it was written in your early environment or family line. The same God who wired you with the ability to *remember* fear also wired you with the ability to rewire toward trust.

The flames of transformation are not only spiritual language; they describe a real rewiring; emotionally, neurologically, even epigenetically. Your body and brain are capable of learning a new story.

The End of Fear (Does Not Mean You Never Feel It)

"The end of fear" does not mean you will never feel afraid again. As long as you are human, in a body, walking through a world of change and uncertainty, waves of fear will still arise:

- before a big conversation,
- when someone you love is in danger,
- when your plans collapse,
- when God feels silent.

The end of fear is not the end of adrenaline, butterflies, or sweaty palms. The end of fear is when fear loses its throne. It is when:

- fear is no longer your main counselor,
- anxiety is no longer the boss of your decisions,
- worst-case scenarios no longer get automatic veto power over your obedience to Love.

You may still hear fear's voice, but you no longer treat it as the voice of God, or of your deepest self. Instead, you might say: "Thank you, fear, for trying to protect me. I see you. But you're not driving today. Love is."

Fear moves from commander to information; something you notice, tend to, and bring into God's presence, but no longer worship.

When Fear Speaks, Ask for Its Story

Because fear is often a story, one of the simplest practices is to let it speak—then listen deeper. When fear rises, you might gently ask:

- "Fear, what are you trying to protect?"

- "What story are you telling me right now?"
- "Where have I felt this before?"
- "Is what you're saying absolutely true?"

Then, in that same moment, turn toward the Presence within and around you and ask: "Love, what is true here? Show me what You see that I cannot see. Help me remember where I am held."

Fear is loud, but it is not truth. The way forward is learning how to work with the mind without being ruled by it. You're not fighting fear with willpower, you're letting Love edit the script.

The bondage of fear can linger where truth has not yet fully dawned. But there is hope beneath the struggle: the soul the Creator breathed into being is not meant for captivity. And in the fullness of time, what is real will be made plain—"every knee will bow and every tongue confess." (Philippians 2:10–11)

What if the next level of freedom is simply noticing the thought... before you believe it?

* * *

Key Insight
Fear is often a story, not a prophecy. It takes a feeling, adds a memory, multiplies it by "always" and "never," and calls the result "truth." Faith does not deny reality; it remembers a deeper Reality—that you are held in Love, even when you do not know the ending. The "end of fear" is not the end of all fearful feelings, but the end of fear's authority to define who you are and what is possible.

Reflection Practice
Write fear's script, then question it. Think of a situation that brings up fear right now. Write down, in a few sentences, the exact story fear is telling you. Don't edit. Let it be dramatic if it wants to.

Then ask:
- "Is this *absolutely* true?"
- "What part of this is assumption?"
- "What do I *not* know yet?"

Finally, write one alternative sentence that leaves room for mystery, like: "I don't know how this will turn out, but I am willing to believe that Love is present and working in ways I can't yet see."

A simple breath prayer for when fear spikes. When you feel fear in your body, place a hand where you feel it most (chest, stomach, throat). Breathe in slowly and pray inwardly: "I am held." Breathe out slowly and pray: "Love is here."

Do this for a minute or two. You're not trying to force the fear away. You're anchoring your nervous system in a deeper truth while the wave moves through.

Bless your fear instead of cursing it. Write a short blessing to your own fear, such as: "Thank you for trying to protect me. I bless you for the times you kept me safe. I release you from leading my life. I choose to be led by Love."

Read it out loud, even if you feel a little silly. Sometimes the end of fear begins with treating it not as a monster to slay, but as a frightened protector that can finally rest.

Remember: "Now we know in part." Take one fear that speaks in absolutes—for example, "This will *never* get better," or "I will *always* be this way." Gently change it to: "Right now it feels like this will never get better. But I admit I only know in part. I open, even slightly, to the possibility of a different ending."

You don't have to feel convinced. You're just opening one window in a room fear has nailed shut.

CHAPTER EIGHT

* * *

THE INNER REALM: STEWARDING THE THOUGHT-LIFE

Most people live their entire lives believing their thoughts are simply "happening" to them, like weather patterns drifting across the mind. But your thought-life is not a passive sky; it is a living garden.

You are the gardener. And every thought is a seed. If this sounds dramatic, that's because it is.

Few things shape the direction of your spiritual journey more than the way you manage your inner dialogue. You can be standing in the presence of God, wrapped in the deepest kind of peace, and still be tormented by a thought. The mind can talk over angels if it wants to.

The truth is simple: You cannot truly live a life of Light while letting your mind run on autopilot.

Jesus hinted at this reality when He said, "As you believe, so shall it be done unto you." Belief begins in thought. Thought becomes perception. Perception becomes experience. Your thoughts are not small. Modern research agrees.

Dr. Joe Dispenza's work on neuroplasticity shows that repeated thoughts literally rewire the brain. Every time you choose a thought aligned with peace instead of fear, compassion instead of judgment, gratitude instead of complaint—you physically reshape the pathways in your brain.

What Scripture calls *renewing of the mind* (Romans 12:2), science calls *rewiring*. And what mystics call *awakening*, Eckhart Tolle calls *observing the thinker*—the ability to step back and become the witness of your thought-life instead of the victim of it.

But here is where things get beautifully simple: You do not have to control your thoughts. You only need to stop letting them control you.

Your thoughts are not dictators. They are suggestions. Some are helpful. Some are nonsense. Some are recycled fears from childhood. Some are wisdom from the deeper Self. Some are simply the brain clearing its throat. The spiritual mistake is believing every thought is true.

Why Thought-Life Matters Spiritually

Your thought-life matters because thoughts shape your perception of God:

- If your mind is filled with fear, you will imagine a fearful God.
- If your mind is filled with shame, you will imagine a condemning God.
- If your mind is filled with Light, you will encounter the God who has always been Light.

Thoughts influence your identity.

Many people treat their thoughts like a mirror. But thoughts are not mirrors, they are megaphones. They don't reflect who you are; they broadcast what you are agreeing with.

Thoughts create your emotional atmosphere A thought is not harmless—it carries a chemical signature. Fearful thoughts activate stress. Grateful thoughts activate peace. Loving thoughts elevate your vibration. Your emotional life is downstream from your thought-life.

Thoughts alter your energy field Your thoughts tune your internal frequency. As Tolle says, "What you think you create, what you feel you attract." Think fearfully long enough, and you begin to attract experiences that validate your fear. Think truthfully long enough, and the world starts reorganizing around clarity.

Thoughts reveal your agreements. Thoughts you repeat become agreements. Agreements become identity. Identity becomes reality.

This is why a single belief can imprison you...or liberate you.

The Three Messages Hidden in Every Thought

Every thought you have is telling you three things:

1. **Something about you**
   - "I'm not enough."--"I am held."
   - "I am alone."—"I am loved."
2. **Something about the world**
   - "Life is dangerous."--"Life is unfolding for me."
3. **Something about God**
   - "He is distant."--"He is within me."
   - "He is silent."--"He is guiding me now."

When a thought is false, all three distortions follow. When a thought is aligned with Light, all three truths unfold.

Practical Guidance: How to Master the Thought-Life

Thought mastery is not about fighting your mind—it's about be-friending it. Your mind is not the enemy. Your mind is more like an enthusiastic puppy trying to protect you... but occasionally chewing up the furniture and barking at things that aren't there.

Here is a simple framework:

1. **Notice the Thought:** Pause. Observe. Don't engage in debate with it. Ask: "Is this thought bringing me into Light or away from it?" Your body will tell you... your peace will tell you...the Spirit will tell you.
2. **Name the Thought: Quietly say,** "This is just a thought." Not identity... not prophecy...not truth... not God, just a thought. Naming it takes away its authority.
3. **Challenge the Thought:** Ask one question: "Is this thought rooted in fear or in love?" Truth always aligns with love. Fear always aligns with illusion. If the thought feels heavy, frantic, urgent, shameful, or contracted, it is not from God. God speaks in peace, not panic.
4. **Replace the Thought:** You cannot "stop" a thought, but you can replace it with a higher one. Examples:
   "I am held."
   "I am guided."
   "This moment is enough."
   "I walk in Light."
   "Love is leading me."

This is how you retrain your internal atmosphere.

5. **Rehearse the Thought Until It Becomes Identity**: Your brain becomes what you repeat. A thought repeated becomes a belief. A belief lived becomes a pattern. A pattern lived becomes identity. Identity becomes experience. This is neuroplasticity...this is renewing the mind...this is *awakening*. Repeating a truth until it becomes familiar is not self-deception—it is self-restoration.

The Thought-Life and the Flow of Spirit

When your inner world becomes ordered:

- peace returns
- discernment sharpens
- intuition awakens
- fear softens
- ego quiets
- light expands

You begin to live in harmony with the Presence within you. You stop forcing life and begin flowing with it. This is what Jesus meant when He said, "The kingdom of God is within you." The inner kingdom is found in the inner realm, and the inner realm is shaped by thought.

Thoughts as Energy: The Vibration of Inner Reality

Every thought carries a frequency. Fear vibrates low and tight. Love vibrates high and expansive. Gratitude harmonizes. Judgment distorts. Peace stabilizes.

Your thoughts create the energetic invitation you send into the world. Modern research in quantum biology suggests that your internal electromagnetic field shifts based on what you think and feel. When Scripture says, "As a man thinks in his heart, so is he," (Proverbs 23:7) it is describing the same principle:

Your thoughts don't just shape your inner world—they shape the field around you.

A thought rooted in fear contracts your energy. A thought rooted in truth expands it.

Your thought-life becomes peaceful when you stop treating every thought like a command. And in that space, Presence becomes more than a concept...it becomes your home. Thoughts are not invisible. They are vibrations that become the architecture of your reality. Choose them wisely.

Choose one ordinary moment today (driving, washing dishes, walking) and be fully there; no commentary.

* * *

Key Insight

Your inner world does not "just happen" to you. Your thought-life is the invisible garden that shapes how you experience God, yourself, and the world. Every repeated thought becomes an agreement, every agreement becomes identity, and identity becomes reality.

Mastering the thought-life isn't about controlling every idea that passes through your mind; it's about recognizing that thoughts are only suggestions, choosing the ones rooted in love and truth, and gently rehearsing them until they become the natural atmosphere of your inner life.

Reflection Practice

Take a moment to notice the story your thoughts have been telling lately.

What are the three phrases you hear most often about yourself, the world, and God?

How do those thoughts feel in your body, tight and fearful, or spacious and peaceful?

If you lived the next five years fully agreeing with those thoughts, who would you become?

Ask the Spirit to highlight one recurring thought that is not aligned with Light. Simply acknowledge: *"This is just a thought, not truth, not identity, not God."* Then listen inwardly for a truer sentence that carries peace.

For the next 7 days, practice this simple 'thought exchange' whenever you notice a heavy or fearful thought:

- **Notice – Pause and say quietly,** *"I'm noticing a fearful thought."* Feel it without judging yourself.
- **Name – Label it:** *"This is just a thought rooted in fear/shame/scarcity."*
- **Exchange – Ask,** *"What is the loving, truthful version of this?"* Then replace it with a higher thought such as:
  - "I am held."…"God is with me in this moment."…"Life is unfolding for my good."
- **Rehearse** – Repeat the new thought slowly, out loud if you can, until your body begins to soften and your breathing steadies.

This simple practice begins to rewire your brain, cleanse the inner atmosphere, and align your thought-life with the Light that has always been within you.

GUIDED MEDITATION

Returning the Mind to Light

Sit comfortably.

Place your hands on your heart. Take one slow breath in.

Let your exhale soften your body.

Bring one troubling thought to mind...do not judge it...do not fight it...just observe it.

Say inwardly: "This is just a thought." Feel the space between *you* and the thought.

Now ask: "Does this thought bring me into Light or away from Light?" Your body will answer.

If it brings contraction: Say gently, "I release this." If it brings expansion: Say softly, "I receive this."

Place your attention on your breath. Let your breath be the bridge between mind and Spirit.

Speak this aloud or silently: "I return my mind to Light."

Breathe once more...let peace rise...let clarity come...let thought become the servant, not the master.

End with gratitude. It rewires the brain faster than anything else.

PART III: FLOW, GUIDANCE & SPIRITUAL ALIGNMENT

As the inner landscape heals, something beautiful happens: you begin to feel Life again—moving, guiding, drawing you forward.

Part III is about learning to live from Presence, not pressure. It's where stillness becomes practical. Where discernment becomes real. Where you stop forcing outcomes and begin to recognize a gentler power at work: the steady guidance of Spirit.

Many people want direction, but few have been taught how guidance actually arrives. It rarely shouts. It often doesn't argue. It doesn't come with panic. The voice of fear pushes. The voice of Love leads.

In this section you'll learn how to recognize that difference—not as a rigid formula, but as a lived relationship. You'll explore what it means to live from Presence, to notice the subtle "language" of Spirit, and to walk in alignment one choice at a time. This is not about becoming mystical or strange. It is about becoming clear. Becoming sincere. Becoming responsive to the Light already within and around you.

Flow isn't passivity. It's cooperation with what is true.

And as you learn to walk this way, your life begins to simplify—not because problems vanish, but because you are no longer divided inside them. You begin moving with integrity. With peace. With quiet courage. You begin to trust that you are being led. Not by control. By light.

What would change if you trusted that guidance is already present—and your role is simply to become still enough to recognize it?

CHAPTER NINE

*** * ***

LIVING FROM PRESENCE

There comes a point on the spiritual path when you realize that managing your thoughts, as important as it is, is still not the deepest thing. You can learn to question fearful stories, shift your inner language, and rewire old patterns—and yet something in you knows: *I am more than the gardener of my mind.*

Presence is that "more."

Presence is the quiet awareness underneath every thought, every feeling, every sensation. It is the you who notices the fear without becoming it, who watches the story without being swallowed by it, who can sit in the middle of inner noise and still sense a deeper stillness that never moves.

In the last chapter, we explored the inner realm of thought—how the mind can be renewed, how stories can be edited, how beliefs shape reality. Living from presence is like stepping one level deeper: instead of only tending the content of your mind, you begin to rest in the One who is aware of the mind at all.

You have already tasted this, even if you didn't name it that way:

- A moment of pure awe when words fell away.
- A quiet breath in the middle of a hard conversation where, for just a second, you knew what to say without rehearsing it.
- A time in prayer when you weren't analyzing, performing, or chasing an answer—you were simply *there*, and somehow that was enough.

That is presence.

Most of us have been trained to live from the surface: from reactions, roles, schedules, and stories. Presence invites you to live from the center. It does not ask you to abandon your life, but to relocate your identity—to shift from *"I am my thoughts, my feelings, my roles"* to *"I am the one in whom these appear."*

This is another truth Jesus was pointing to when He said, "The kingdom of God is within you." Not a far-off realm you visit after death, but an inner atmosphere you can become aware of in this very moment.

"What if the deepest part of me is not something I have to build, but something I have to notice?"

Living from presence is learning to answer that question with your life.

Stillness: The Doorway to Presence

Teachers like Eckhart Tolle often describe presence in one simple word: *stillness.* Not a forced silence, not an empty mind you strain to maintain, but the natural quiet that appears when you stop chasing every thought and let this moment be as *It Is.*

Stillness is not something you manufacture. It is what remains when you are no longer arguing with reality. You may notice it in the gap between breaths. In the pause before you answer. In the simple act of feeling your own aliveness without needing to label it.

Tolle points again and again to this inner stillness—not as a technique, but as the living doorway to who you really are. In those moments when you are just *here*, not replaying the past, not rehearsing the future...you are closer to your true self than you realize. You haven't disappeared; the noise has.

From a Christian lens, this stillness is not empty space; it is shared space. It is where "Christ in you" is most easily recognized. It is the atmosphere where the Spirit's whisper can finally be heard beneath the mind's volume.

"What happens if, just for a moment, I stop trying to fix this and simply become still with it before God?"

Again and again, the answer is the same: you find that Presence was here before the problem, remains with you in the middle of it. And will outlast every story your mind tells about it.

Practice: A Simple Stillness Prayer (5 Minutes)

You don't have to escape your life to touch stillness. You just have to give this moment your full attention.

Take your seat. Sit comfortably, feet on the floor or legs relaxed. Let your hands rest gently in your lap. You don't have to "sit perfectly"— just be supported.

Notice your breath. Close your eyes if you'd like. Feel one natural inhale... and one natural exhale. Don't force anything. Let your breathing be exactly as it is.

Feel your body here. Notice the weight of your body on the chair. Notice the contact of your feet with the floor. If your mind starts commenting, that's okay. Simply return to: *"Here I am."*

Invite the Presence. Quietly pray, in your own words or something like: "God, I am here. You are here. Let me rest in Your presence." No need to perform. Just mean it as much as you can.

Let thoughts come and go. Thoughts will arise. They always do. Instead of chasing them, imagine they are clouds passing across a wide sky. You are not the cloud. You are the sky. If you get lost in a thought, gently return to your breath and the awareness of God-with-you.

Rest in the silence between. For a few moments, notice the small spaces: the pause between breaths, the quiet between thoughts, the stillness underneath sensations. You don't have to *make* anything happen. You are simply *being* with the One who is.

Close with gratitude. After 3–5 minutes, take one deeper breath. Whisper a simple thank you: "Thank You for being here, even when I forget." Open your eyes and carry that quiet with you into whatever comes next.

Reflection: What did I notice in those few minutes of stillness— about my body, my thoughts, or the sense of God's presence? What changes in my day when I pause like this, even briefly?

Witness Consciousness and the "I Am"

Presence is not an abstract spiritual state; it is the simple recognition that you are the one who *sees*.

You are not the rush of thoughts.
You are not the storm of emotions.
You are not the roles you play or the labels you've collected.

You are the awareness in which all of those appear and disappear.

This is sometimes called *witness consciousness*—the quiet sense of "I am here" that remains even when your thoughts change, your feelings shift, and your circumstances move from one season to another.

Scripture hints at this mystery when God reveals Himself to Moses as "I AM." In the New Testament, Paul says, "It is no longer I who live, but Christ lives in me." There is a deep resonance here: the truest "I" in you is rooted in the One who simply *Is*.

When you live from presence, you are not trying to erase your personality or escape your humanity. You are letting your thoughts, emotions, and actions flow from a deeper center—the "I am" in you that is grounded in God's life, not in fear's stories.

"What if the most honest thing I can say about myself in any moment is simply: 'I am here, with God, right now'?"

Living Presence in Ordinary Moments

It's easy to think presence belongs only in long, quiet mornings and silent retreats. But if presence doesn't work in traffic, staff meetings, parenting, and hospital waiting rooms, it's not the kind of presence Jesus modeled. Presence is not about removing yourself *from* life…it is about bringing your whole self *into* life.

Here are simple ways presence can show up in an ordinary day:

- **One conscious breath before you speak.** Before answering a difficult email, having a hard conversation, or responding to a text, pause for one slow inhale and exhale. Let that breath be your reminder: *I don't have to react. I can respond from Presence.*

- **Feeling your feet on the ground.** When anxiety spikes, gently shift attention to the sensation of your feet touching the floor or your body on the chair. This anchors you back into the present moment instead of letting your mind sprint into imagined futures.
- **Naming the moment. Quietly say, "Right now, I am __."** "Right now, I am driving.", "Right now, I am washing dishes.", "Right now, I am listening to this person."

  Naming pulls you out of mental time-travel and back into what is actually happening with God.

- **Inviting God into the middle, not just the edges**. Instead of waiting for a "holy" moment to pray, whisper short prayers throughout the day: "You are with me in this phone call.", "You with me in this hallway walk.", "You are with me as I make this decision."

  Presence deepens when you stop dividing life into "spiritual" and "everything else."

Over time, these small practices begin to change your inner posture. You stop living as someone chasing God from a distance and start living as someone walking with God in each step, breath, and interaction.

When Presence Meets Pain

Living from presence does not mean you stop feeling pain, sadness, or frustration. It means you no longer face them alone, or only from the level of the mind. When you meet pain from presence, something shifts:

- You can feel what you feel without building a whole identity around it.
- You can let grief move through you without deciding it is the final word.
- You can notice fear, shame, or anger and still remember, even faintly: *"I am held. God is here with me in this."*

Presence does not erase your humanity. It dignifies it. In presence, tears are not a sign that you've failed spiritually. They are simply part of what this moment contains...with God in the middle of it.

Presence is the doorway through which guidance is felt. From here, we begin learning how Spirit communicates; quietly, clearly, personally.

May you grow fluent in the gentle ways God speaks—through peace, clarity, and love.

* * *

Key Insight

Living from presence is not about achieving a rare spiritual state; it is about returning, again and again, to the quiet awareness of "I am here, and God is here."

Thoughts will still come. Feelings will still rise and fall. Circumstances will still change. But presence shifts your identity:
- from the storm -> to the sky,
- from the story -> to the One who sees,
- from chasing God "out there" -> to recognizing God *here*—in this breath, in this body, in this exact moment.

Reflection Practice

When in my recent life have I most clearly tasted presence—those moments where I felt deeply here, even if just for a second?

What are the main ways I abandon the present moment—worry, replaying the past, constant distraction, overthinking?

How might one simple practice (a breath, a short prayer, feeling my feet) help me return to presence during my normal day?

What changes in how I see God if I begin to trust that His Presence is here in this moment, not waiting for me somewhere else?

CHAPTER TEN

* * *

LEARNING THE LANGUAGE OF SPIRIT

There comes a moment in every awakening when a new question rises to the surface: *"If the Spirit is really this close...how do I know when I'm actually being led?"*

Presence (Chapter 9) teaches you that the Holy One is here, not distant. But as that becomes real, another layer of longing appears. You don't just want to *be* with God, you want to *walk* with the Presence. You want to respond, to follow, to move in step with something wiser than your personality and more loving than your fear. And then the mind jumps in:

"God, is that You... or just my anxiety rehearsing?" "Is that the Spirit... or last night's pizza?"

"Is this an intuition... or am I just making things up?"

If you've ever had those thoughts, congratulations. You're not spiritually broken. You're simply waking up to the art of discernment.

Learning the language of Spirit is not about becoming a mystical codebreaker, chasing secret signs in every cloud formation. It is about growing in sensitivity to a Presence that is already speaking, in ways that are often quieter, kinder, and simpler than the mind expects.

"What if guidance is less about decoding messages and more about recognizing a relationship?"

Why Guidance Often Feels Confusing

If the One who made you is Love, and Love desires to guide, why does guidance sometimes feel so complicated? Part of the difficulty is that most of us were trained to listen almost exclusively to the loudest channel inside us...the mind.

The mind loves:

- analysis,
- control,
- certainty, and preferably a detailed five-year plan.

Spirit often moves in:

- nudges,
- peace,
- resonance,
- step-by-step light.

No wonder there's tension. On top of that, we carry old fears about "missing God's will", pressure to "never make a wrong move", and images of God who is more like a strict boss than a patient Guide.

If you secretly believe that one wrong turn will permanently eject you from your destiny, of course you'll be terrified of making decisions. Fear of getting it wrong will drown out the very guidance you're longing to hear.

But what if guidance is less like a single narrow tightrope and more like a living conversation with Divine Love, who can re-route, redeem, and re-weave even your detours?

What if the question is not, *"Did I get the one perfect path exactly right?"* but,

"Am I walking with the One who can lead me from here?"

The Subtlety of Spirit

When the prophet Elijah went looking for the Eternal's voice, he encountered a wind so strong it shattered rocks, an earthquake that shook the ground, and a fire that blazed with power. But the text is clear. The Holy One was:

- not in the wind,
- not in the earthquake,
- not in the fire.

Then came what many translations call "a still small voice"—others render it "a gentle whisper," or literally, "the sound of sheer silence."

That's often how guidance comes:

- Not as a booming command.
- Not as a neon sign.
- Not as a 47-point to-do list from heaven.

But as:

- a quiet clarity,
- a sense of inner "rightness" or dissonance,
- a peace that doesn't entirely make sense on paper,
- a simple phrase that lands in the heart with weight and gentleness at the same time.

This can be frustrating to the ego, which would like the Almighty to email a PDF with your exact life plan attached.

Yet there's wisdom in the subtlety. If guidance were always loud and overwhelming, you'd never learn to pay attention. You'd obey from pressure, not love. Subtlety invites relationship. It asks you to lean in, to listen, to keep returning to the Presence—not just for answers, but for companionship.

"Am I seeking guidance as information to control my future, or as an invitation to walk more closely with the Living Presence in the present?"

Science, Intuition, and the Nervous System

"Language of Spirit" can sound vague or mystical, but even science quietly nods in this direction. Your body and brain are not just reacting to life; they are constantly reading it.

Neuroscience tells us that your brain is a pattern-recognition engine. Your nervous system is always scanning for safety and meaning. Much of your processing happens below conscious awareness *before* it surfaces as a "sense," "gut feeling," or "something I just know."

Psychologists talk about intuition as "rapid, unconscious processing of information." That doesn't mean every hunch is holy. But it does mean there's more going on than pure logic.

Contemplative practices like stillness, breath, prayer, and honest self-awareness have been shown to:

- calm the stress response,
- increase coherence between heart and brain,
- and heighten your sensitivity to subtle signals in your body and environment.

The Spirit doesn't bypass your biology. Ruach works *through* it. So when you feel a deep, grounded peace about a choice that makes no sense on paper, or a quiet unease about something that looks perfect externally, it may not be "just your imagination". It may be your whole being—body, brain, and spirit—tuning into a deeper reality.

Guidance is not always a voice in words. Sometimes it is the way truth settles in your nervous system.

Ruach and Shema: Hearing With the Whole Self

This is where the Hebrew language becomes a beautiful teacher. In English, we split things up: spirit...breath...wind.

In Hebrew, a single word holds them together, ruach. *Ruach* means *breath*, *wind*, and *spirit* all at once.

When Scripture talks about the Spirit of God moving, filling, hovering, it's using this word: Ruach Elohim. The image is not of a distant force, but of the very breath and movement of God, like wind you can't see but can feel, like breath that animates you from the inside.

Jesus echoed this when He said, "The wind blows where it wills... so it is with everyone born of the Spirit." Spirit moves like wind: real, present, but not controlled by human schedules.

Another key Hebrew word is shema. *Shema* is usually translated as *hear* or *listen*: "Hear, O Israel..." (Deuteronomy 6:4).

But in Hebrew, *shema* is not just hearing sounds. It carries the sense of: listen, pay attention, take in, and respond/obey.

To *shema* is to hear with the whole self; ears, heart, and action. From that perspective, "learning the language of Spirit" is really about learning to shema the ruach: to notice the subtle "wind" of the Divine moving in your life, to let that movement reach your heart, and to respond in real ways, however small.

Guidance, in this sense, is not just God "talking" and you trying to decode. It is a living exchange of breath: Ruach Elohim breathing life, wisdom, and nudges into you...you breathing back honesty, willingness, and response.

"What would it look like for me to 'hear' the Holy One with my whole being—not just my ears and intellect, but my heart, body, and choices?"

How Spirit Commonly Speaks

If you grew up hearing dramatic stories of burning bushes, angelic visitations, and booming voices from the sky, everyday guidance can feel... underwhelming. But most of the time, the Holy Spirit speaks in ways that are repeatable, gentle, and woven right into your ordinary life.

Here are some of the most common "channels." None of them are a formula. All of them are invitations.

Peace vs. Pressure: One of the simplest indicators of guidance is the difference between peace and pressure. Peace doesn't always mean "this will be easy." It means "this is aligned."

Pressure feels like:

- "Hurry up or you'll miss it."
- "If you don't decide *right now*, God will be mad."
- "Do this or else."

Peace feels more like:

- "You still may feel nervous, but something in you can breathe."
- "You don't have all the answers, but you know your next honest step."
- "You don't feel bullied; you feel gently drawn."

The Spirit's guidance may challenge you, stretch you, and even scare you a little. But Divine Love will not bully you.

"Does this 'guidance' feel like I'm being lovingly led—or desperately threatened?"

Scripture Coming Alive: For many followers of Jesus, one of the primary ways Spirit speaks is through Scripture, not as random verses dropped like fortune cookies, but as living words that arrive with uncanny timing and clarity. You might:

- read a familiar passage that suddenly lands with new depth,
- hear a phrase echo in your heart across multiple days, sermons, or conversations,
- sense a particular story mirroring exactly what you're wrestling with.

On paper, it's ink and pages. In your spirit, it becomes food.

The same text that once felt flat suddenly reads *you*. This isn't about twisting verses to say whatever you want; it's about letting the Spirit of Christ use timeless words to speak into a very specific now.

Desires Refined by Love: Not every desire is selfish. Not every longing is a distraction. As you heal, your desires themselves begin to change. Things that once attracted you lose their grip; things that once bored you begin to glow. The Spirit often guides by shaping what you genuinely want:

- a pull toward a certain kind of work or service,
- compassion for a particular group of people,
- a growing hunger for truth, integrity, beauty, or freedom.

The ego's desires tend to orbit around:

- image,
- control,
- comparison,
- and "What will they think?"

Desires being purified by Love tend to orbit around:

- love,
- contribution,
- authenticity,
- and "Who can I be for others in this?"

Guidance may be hiding inside the very longings you keep dismissing as "just me."

Wise Voices and Holy Conversations: Ruach also loves to speak through other people—often when they don't even realize they're being used that way. A friend says one simple sentence that slices through your confusion. A mentor asks the one question you were avoiding. A child blurts out the truth with disarming innocence. Sometimes you hear your own mouth say something to someone else and realize, *"That was for me, too."*

Of course, not every opinion is the voice of the Holy One. Discernment means noticing:

- Does this resonate with the peace of Christ in me?
- Does it align with love, truth, and what I already know of God's character?
- Does it confirm something I've been sensing, or contradict it with fear and shame?

The Good Shepherd rarely guides you into something that requires you to betray your deepest sense of what is good and loving.

Creation, Symbol, and "Coincidence": You don't need to turn every cloud into a prophetic sign. (If the cloud looks like an elephant, it probably just looks like an elephant.)

But creation is not mute. There are moments when:

- a sunrise,
- a tree bending in the wind,
- a hawk circling overhead,
- or a perfectly timed "coincidence" arrives in a way that bypasses your intellect and lands directly in the heart.

You feel seen. You feel spoken to. You feel, even for a moment, that the veil between "spiritual" and "physical" is much thinner than you thought.

You don't have to chase these moments. Simply notice them. Let gratitude be your response. Guidance often rides on the back of gratitude.

Doors That Open... and Doors That Don't: Sometimes the clearest guidance is circumstantial. You pray, sense a direction, take steps—

and suddenly: a way opens that you could not have engineered, or a door slams shut no matter how hard you push.

A closed door is not always a punishment. It may be protection, redirection, or simply timing. An open door is not always an automatic "yes". It may be an opportunity to practice discernment. Guidance is learning to ask:

- "Holy Spirit, is this door for now, or just to show me what's possible?"
- "If it's closed, is it 'not ever' or 'not yet'?"

The Persistent Nudge: One of the most reliable forms of guidance is the nudge that won't go away...you've tried to ignore it... you've explained it away...you've told the Lord, "Ask someone else". And yet, it returns:

- "Call this person."
- "Forgive them."
- "Let this go."
- "Take this step."
- "Rest."

It doesn't scream. It doesn't threaten. It just keeps gently knocking on the same door in your heart. The longer you walk with Christ, the more you recognize that tone. It's not nagging. It's Love.

Things God Probably Didn't Say
A little humor can help us loosen the grip of fear-based "guidance." If you hear something like this inside, you can almost certainly cross it off the list:

- "If you don't figure out My will perfectly, I'm done with you."
- "Buy that thing you absolutely can't afford. I'll be so impressed."
- "Never rest. Exhaustion brings Me glory."
- "If you feel peace, it's probably a trap. Choose the most miserable option; that's the holy one."
- "I'll lead you, but only if you're 100% sure it's Me first."

Guidance may lead you into hard things. It may ask for sacrifice. It may stretch you way beyond your comfort. But it will not: mock you, belittle you, shame you, or delight in your confusion.

The voice that sounds like an abusive coach in your head is not the voice of the Good Shepherd, the One Jesus revealed as Abba. Sometimes the holiest thing you can do is laugh and say, "Yeah... that doesn't sound like God at all."

Spirit, Ego, or Fear? A Simple Discernment Grid

When you're unsure whether a "word," idea, or nudge is from Spirit, from your ego, or from fear, it can help to ask:

What is the emotional tone?

- Spirit: calm, clear, steady—even if challenging.
- Ego: dramatic, self-centered, obsessed with image.
- Fear: frantic, contracted, panicky, all-or-nothing.

What is this leading me *toward*?

- Spirit: love, truth, humility, deeper connection.
- Ego: impressing others, winning, being "special."
- Fear: hiding, shrinking, controlling, avoiding.

How does this align with what I know of Jesus?

- *Would the Jesus who: welcomes the broken, confronts pretended holiness, lays down His life, and calls you "beloved", say this, in this way, for this purpose?*

If the "guidance" contradicts the character of Christ, you can safely lay it down. Guidance is not usually thunder, it is often a steady nudge toward what is true. And the real test of guidance is not what you hear, but how you walk.

Consider: *"If I imagined this guidance being spoken by the most loving, wise, and truthful Presence I can conceive of, does it still sound the same?"*

* * *

Key Insight

Learning the language of Spirit is not about cracking a secret code; it is about growing in relationship with the One who is already speaking. Guidance is usually: quiet, not flashy; peaceful, not panicked; inviting, not coercive.

Ruach works *with* your biology, history, and uniqueness:

- through peace in your nervous system,
- through desires refined by love,
- through Scripture that comes alive,
- through wise voices,
- through closed doors and opened paths,
- through nudges that simply will not go away.

The question is rarely, "Is God speaking?" but more often, "Am I willing to slow down, listen with my whole being, and respond to what I already sense from Spirit, from Christ within, from the Presence that loves me?"

I realize some of this may sound redundant or like plain common sense. But unless you've been living under a rock, you've probably noticed that common sense is trampled daily; and even the most aware can get swept up in the herd from time to time.

Reflection Practice

Looking Back: When in my life do I most clearly remember being guided—where I sensed a "rightness" or warning that proved true in hindsight?

Tone Check: Think of a current decision or situation where I'm seeking guidance. The inner voices around it; do they sound more like Spirit, ego, or fear?

Ruach & Shema in Me: How might I "hear with my whole self" this week...paying attention not just with my mind, but with my body, emotions, and choices?

One Concrete Experiment: What is one small nudge I already sense but have been ignoring? What is one simple step I can take to respond?

CHAPTER ELEVEN

* * *

WALKING IN ALIGNMENT

"My yoke is easy, and My burden is light."

Hearing the language of Spirit is one thing. Walking with the Spirit is another. You can have powerful moments of guidance, deep experiences of Presence in stillness, and genuine clarity in prayer—then lose it all by 9:15 a.m. when your email app loads. That's where alignment moves from idea to lifestyle.

In Part I, we talked about alignment as inner coherence: your heart, mind, and life beginning to point in the same direction. Here, we're talking about walking alignment: how you move through your actual day—meetings, traffic, hard conversations, text messages—with your inner and outer life still tethered to the same Center.

Jesus put it this way: "Come to Me... Take My yoke upon you and learn from Me...for My yoke is easy and My burden is light."

A *yoke* was a way two animals walked side by side, sharing the weight of the work. Walking in alignment is learning to live *yoked* to Christ— letting your steps sync with His rhythm instead of being dragged by fear, urgency, and everyone else's expectations.

"If my day were a walk, who or what usually sets the pace: Spirit, fear, or my calendar?"

What Walking in Alignment Feels Like (And What It Doesn't)

Let's start with what it *doesn't* feel like. Walking in alignment does not mean: every day is serene and perfectly scheduled, you never get stressed, you float through life like a holy hummingbird. In fact, some of your most aligned days may still look chaotic on the outside.

Alignment is less about what's happening around you and more about who *you're being* as it happens. When you're walking in alignment, life still happens, but something in you isn't fighting the whole thing.

It often feels like:

- The right kind of effort—You may be busy, but you're not carrying everything alone. There's a "shared yoke" sense—work is still work, but it's not crushing.
- Quicker recoveries— You still get thrown off, but you come back to center faster. You don't spiral for days over what once would have wrecked you.
- Congruence—You're not saying "yes" with your mouth while your spirit screams "no." Your decisions increasingly line up with what you know in your deepest place.
- Quiet peace under the noise—The surface might be loud, but somewhere underneath, there's a steady river of "I am held."

When you're *out* of alignment, it tends to feel like:

- Constant urgency, even when nothing is actually on fire.
- Saying yes because you're afraid, not because you're called.
- Resentment building under "service."
- A low-grade sense of "I'm betraying myself again."

"If I'm honest, where in my life do I feel that quiet sense of 'I'm out of step with myself and with God'?"

Resistance vs. Surrender: The Two Ways of Walking

There are really only two ways to walk through a day:

- <u>In resistance</u> – pushing, forcing, gripping, trying to control everything and everyone.
- <u>In surrender</u> – not passivity, but an active willingness to move with the Light instead of against it.

Resistance sounds like:

- "I have to hold this all together."
- "This day must go exactly as I've planned."
- "If they don't respond the way I want, everything is ruined."

Surrender sounds more like:

- "I will do what I can, from a place of peace—and I will trust the rest."
- "If plans change, I will look for where the Spirit is still moving."
- "I am willing to be led, even if it means a different route than I had in mind."

One of the funniest (and humbling) parts of awakening is realizing how often we've prayed, "Your will be done," while secretly meaning, "as long as Your will is basically my will, with better parking."

Walking in alignment means you slowly shift from: "Bless what I've already decided," to "Shape my desires, then guide my steps."

The Science of Flow and the Spiritual Walk

Psychologists sometimes talk about flow state—a mental and emotional state where you're fully immersed in what you're doing, time seems to shift. And your actions feel almost effortless, even if what you're doing is challenging.

Research tells us that in flow:

- The brain quiets certain self-critical regions.
- Attention becomes focused yet relaxed.
- Performance improves without the feeling of strain.

Sound familiar? Spiritually, walking in alignment often has a similar "flow" quality...not because life is easy, but because you're not fighting yourself every second. You could say, flow is what happens when your gifts, focus, and environment align. Walking in the Spirit is what happens when your heart, will, and the guidance of Divine Love align.

When your nervous system is constantly in fight-or-flight, everything feels like resistance. When you practice stillness, breath, gratitude, and honest alignment, the nervous system shifts into a more coherent rhythm. Your body becomes more available for guidance. Your mind stops screaming long enough to notice the next step.

You're not less human in alignment. You're more *integrated*...spirit, soul, and body walking together in one direction.

"What daily practices help my system shift from chronic urgency into a posture where I can actually sense guidance?"

A Personal Story: Learning to Walk the Day with God

There came a point in my spiritual journey when I started to quietly despise the busyness of my life. The constant rush, the noise, the endless to-do lists; I could feel how out of sync they were with what the Spirit was stirring in me. Thankfully, Grace was moving me and I was beginning to notice gentle nudges from the Holy Spirit to make changes.

My prayer life slowly shifted. Mornings became sacred. What began as a few minutes of prayer grew into longer stretches of contemplative stillness…much longer than I ever imagined I could sit without "doing" anything. I was being awakened into that Stillness, that sacred Silence.

But a frustration rose alongside the beauty: I didn't know how to carry that Presence into the chaos of my workday.

So I started setting alarms on my phone; little reminders throughout the day to stop, breathe, and give thanks. Those pauses helped, but I soon became dissatisfied with brief moments of awareness. I *knew* there was more. I sensed that I could, and should, be living *in* the moments themselves, in the present Now, as Eckhart Tolle describes.

There was an intense desire in me to walk in peace, to move in harmony and love, to choose instant forgiveness, to let go of judgment and see through the lens Jesus modeled so perfectly. I resonated deeply with Frank Laubach's longing in *Letters by a Modern Mystic*…to walk with God every minute of every waking hour.

And under all of this, I was constantly yearning to fully realize the power and love within me that Paul proclaims in 2 Timothy 1:7.

I wish I could say I've mastered this…I haven't.

But I *can* say that through intentionally practicing this focus, especially in the middle of the chaos that many days bring, I am much better at it than I used to be. I recover presence more quickly. I return to peace more often. And I will continue to aspire and grow as long as I'm on this beautiful journey.

I believe it is imperative for us to have and maintain a growth mind-set: not "I have arrived," but "I am learning to walk with God, step by step, moment by moment, realizing the light within".

"Where in my own day am I most aware of walking with God, and where do I usually forget?"

Practice: Following the Peace

One of the simplest and most powerful ways to walk in alignment is what I call "Follow the Peace." It's not about chasing comfort. It's about letting the peace of Christ be the "referee" in your inner world. Here's a simple way to practice it:

Bring the choice into the Light: Think of a decision you're facing—a conversation, a commitment, a change, even how to spend your evening. Name it honestly before God: "Here is what I'm considering..."

Hold each option in stillness: One at a time, imagine yourself taking that path. Not just the outcome—imagine the *living of it*. Ask inwardly: "What happens to my inner atmosphere as I picture this?" Do you feel:

- more open or more tight?
- more honest or more performative?
- more like you're moving with Love or performing for fear?

Notice where the deeper peace resides: Peace here is not "this feels easy." It is, "Even if this is hard, something in me knows this is true."

Choose in alignment with that peace, and keep listening: Walking in alignment is rarely a one-and-done decision. It's a series of small "yeses" to where peace keeps pointing.

Your actions reveal the intensity of your desire. When a desire is aligned with God, it asks for more than good intentions; it asks for fervent follow-through and honest accountability. Not striving to earn love, but cooperating with love: taking the next faithful step, again and again.

I have never seen a soul genuinely seek truth without tasting some measure of it—no matter what tradition they began in. The Light honors sincerity. And since the veil has been torn, why live as if distance is still the norm between Creator and creation?

Sometimes what blocks us isn't sin as much as attachment to words—labels we cling to, arguments we rehearse, conclusions we refuse to revisit. Words can become mental walls. Truth makes them windows.

Sometimes peace will lead you *into* a hard conversation. Sometimes peace will say, "Rest instead of proving yourself."

Sometimes peace will nudge, "Let this go. You don't need to fix it."

Over time you begin to recognize: *This is what the Shepherd's voice feels like in me.*

Micro-Alignments: The Small Steps That Shape a Day

Most of walking in alignment is made of very small choices. Not dramatic spiritual heroics, just micro-alignments that keep you pointed toward love. Examples:

• Before reacting, breathe once. One deep breath gives Spirit a chance to step between your trigger and your response.

• Align your "yes" and your "no." Before committing, quietly ask: *"If I say yes to this, what am I saying no to? If I say no, what does that protect in me?"*

• Treat interruptions as possible invitations. Not every interruption is holy—but some of them are. Ask: *"Is this an invitation to love, or just noise?"*

• Schedule with soul, not only with efficiency. Instead of cramming every space, leave intentional gaps in your day...breathing spaces where you can re-align.

You don't become aligned by one huge spiritual moment. You become aligned by a thousand tiny turns toward the same Light.

A Gentle Quantum Parable

Physicists tell us that in the quantum world, particles exist in a cloud of possibilities until they are "observed." Then one reality collapses into being. Without trying to turn this into a science sermon, there's a parable hidden here. Every moment of your day carries multiple possible ways of responding:

Alignment becomes real when it shows up in choices, not just insights. And when those choices become consistent, you begin to recognize something beautiful: you are being led.

- the fearful reaction,
- the ego-protecting reaction,
- the numb reaction,
- and the aligned response that flows from your deepest self in God.

You "collapse" one of those possibilities into reality each time you choose.

Walking in alignment is not about perfection. It's about choosing, as often as you can see it, the response that reflects Love instead of fear.

Alignment becomes real when it shows up in choices, not just insights. And when choices become consistent, you begin to recognize something beautiful: you are being led.

Before your next decision, take one breath and ask, *"Does this expand light, or reinforce fear?"*

* * *

Key Insight

Walking in alignment is not about having a perfectly ordered life; it is about walking with a rightly ordered heart. It is the daily, ordinary miracle of letting the peace of Christ, not fear, urgency, or ego, set your pace and shape your responses.

You will drift, you will forget, and you will have days where you only notice your missteps at the end of the night. But every honest return is alignment. Every small "yes" to peace is walking in the Spirit. Every step taken with the Presence; in traffic, in hallways, in laundry rooms, in meetings, becomes part of the quiet revolution of a life yoked to Love.

Reflection Practice

My Current Pace:
If I described the pace of my life in one word, what would it be? (Rushed, frantic, steady, intentional, scattered, yoked)

Peace as Referee:
Think of one decision or relationship where I feel out of alignment. What happens in my body and spirit when I bring it into stillness and ask: *"Where does the deeper peace reside?"*

One Micro-Alignment:
What is one small daily practice I can adopt this week (a breath, a short prayer, a pause before replying, a gap in my schedule) to help me walk more in step with the Spirit?

Honest Confession:
Finish this sentence in my journal or prayer:

"Holy Spirit, here is where I feel out of step with You, and here is my desire for how I want to walk instead..."

CHAPTER TWELVE

* * *

BEING LED BY LIGHT

The Path That Forms Under Your Feet

There is a difference between walking in alignment and being led by Light. Walking in alignment (Chapter 11) is about how you move through *today*: your pace, your responses, your breath, your yes and no. Being led by Light is about something larger and slower:

- How your *life* is guided.
- How callings emerge.
- How doors open and close.
- How the path you could not see slowly reveals itself beneath your feet.

It's one thing to feel God in a quiet morning. It's another to trust the Holy One with a whole decade.

"Do I believe the Presence only meets me in moments, or is actually guiding the long arc of my life?"

The Rhythm Beneath the Noise

Most of us were taught to think of life as something we have to manage, control, and plan within an inch of its existence—or it will fall apart and God will be "disappointed."

But underneath all the noise, there is a quieter truth: there is a rhythm to life that reveals itself the moment we stop trying to direct the current and begin allowing it to carry us. The kingdom does not arrive through force; it unfolds through trust. Divine guidance rarely shouts. It nudges, whispers, and draws us forward with a peace that surpasses understanding.

We're meant to navigate that flow using our inner GPS—and no, not the Global Positioning System. I'm talking about the deeper guidance that arises from within, the quiet compass of God, Presence, and Stillness that is always ready to lead us when we ask. When we listen to that inner alignment, we find ourselves moving with life rather than against it.

This is the essence of walking by faith. Faith is not blind optimism; it is the deep knowing that the same Presence animating the universe is also animating you. According to your faith it will be given to you— not because God is withholding blessings, but because faith opens the channel through which divine flow can be recognized and received.

Wind carries truth. Its direction cannot be controlled, only sensed. In the same way, the Spirit moves where it wills, and those who awaken learn to feel the subtle shifts of guidance within their own being. Sometimes the flow carries you forward; sometimes it redirects you entirely. But every movement is purposeful.

When resistance falls away, life itself becomes a collaboration with the Divine. The more you trust the inner GPS—Presence, Stillness, that unmistakable resonance of peace—the more clearly you recognize that guidance has always been there, not forcing...not demanding...simply inviting you into the current of what already is.

Your inner GPS doesn't give turn-by-turn instructions for the next fifteen years. It doesn't say, "In 4.5 months, make a sharp left into a brand-new vocation."

It works more like this:

- "For now, go this way."
- "Now, pause here."
- "Now, release that."
- "Now, take this step."

And only later do you look back and realize, *"Oh. That was a path."*

Ask: *"Where have I already seen a path appear in hindsight that I could not see at the time?"*

Why We Want a Map Instead of a Guide

Let's be honest: most of us would prefer a detailed map over a living Guide. We'd happily receive a 40-page PDF from Heaven, a five-year plan with color-coding, and a guarantee that if we follow it, nothing too painful will happen and we will always understand what's going on.

Instead, we get a Person, we get Presence, we get Light... one step at a time. There's a reason for this. If you had the whole map:

- you'd try to skip the parts you don't like,
- you'd cling to the outcomes instead of the One leading you,
- and you'd probably spend more time arguing with page 7 than living page 1.

A map encourages control. A Guide invites trust. Being led by Light means learning to say:

- "I don't see the whole story...but I know who is walking with me."
- "I don't understand this detour...but I choose to believe it is not wasted."
- "I don't know the outcome...but I can see the next faithful step."

The Brain That Hates Not Knowing (And Why Faith Feels Hard)

Modern neuroscience tells us your brain is a prediction machine. It's constantly trying to answer three questions:

- *What's happening?*
- *What will happen next?*
- *How do I stay safe?*

Uncertainty feels like a threat. That's why waiting, not knowing, and "living by faith" can feel so physically uncomfortable.

Your nervous system is wired to prefer:

- clear expectations,
- repeatable patterns,
- and outcomes it can predict.

Spirit, however, often leads in a way that:

- disrupts old patterns,

- invites new ways of seeing,
- and asks you to trust what you cannot yet predict.

So if you feel tension in seasons of transition, you're not "failing spiritually." You're bumping into your biology.

This is where gentle practices—breath, stillness, honest prayer, gratitude—help shift your system from "threat mode" to "trust mode," so you can sense the quiet leading underneath the noise.

Faith doesn't require you to shut off your brain. It invites your mind to relax its demand for total control and let Love hold the unknown with you.

Pause: *"Am I asking God to remove all uncertainty, or to meet me inside it?"*

Signs You Are Being Led (Even When You Don't Feel It)

How do you know when you're actually being led by Light and not just wandering? It rarely looks as glamorous as we imagine. More often, it looks like this:

- Right doors at the wrong time (in your opinion). An opportunity appears when you feel unready, yet deep down you sense, "This is for me."
- Wrong doors at the right time (in your opinion). You want something badly. You prepare, knock, push...and the door simply won't open. Years later, you see why.
- Threads that keep returning. A theme, calling, or desire keeps resurfacing through different seasons—through conversations, books, Scripture, inner nudges. You can ignore it for a while, but it keeps circling back.
- The "accidental" alignment of circumstances. You meet the right person at a random event. You overhear the exact sentence you needed. A book "happens" to cross your path at the perfect time.
- A growing sense of "I couldn't have orchestrated that." Looking back, you see a series of convergences you weren't smart enough to plan.

Being led by Light is not about everything going "smoothly." It's about noticing an underlying Intelligence, a gentle choreography, that keeps weaving through your story, even through delays, losses, and detours.

Detours, Delays, and the God of Rerouting

Have you ever missed a turn while using GPS? It doesn't scream, "You absolute disaster! Journey over." It simply says, "Recalculating..." and finds another route from where you are. Divine guidance is like that— only kinder.

Many of us imagine that one wrong relationship, one bad decision, or one missed opportunity has permanently knocked us out of "God's will," and now we're on some second-rate backup plan, while heaven sadly shrugs.

But if God's guidance can be thwarted by your worst decision, then your mistakes are more powerful than God. They're not. The Holy One is not just the God of straight lines. The Holy One is the God of rerouting.

Will there be consequences to certain choices? Of course. Will some paths take longer than they needed to? Probably. Can anything finally separate you from Love's ability to lead you from *here*? No.

Being led by Light is not about having a flawless record. It's about learning to say, in any moment, "Okay. From *here*, lead me."

Consider: *"Am I more focused on the turn I missed, or on the Light that is still willing to guide me now?"*

The Path That Forms Under Your Feet

One of the most beautiful discoveries on this journey is that the path doesn't fully appear before you walk. It appears as you walk. You take a step:

- to forgive when you'd rather resent,
- to tell the truth when it would be easier to hide,
- to follow a nudge that doesn't yet make sense,
- to move in love when fear wants to freeze. And that step reveals the next stone in the river.

This is why Jesus so often said, "Come, follow Me," instead of, "Sit still while I give you a detailed presentation about the next thirty years of your life." Following is how the path appears.

You may have noticed this already:

- You committed to a small act of obedience, and through that act you met someone who shaped your journey.
- You said yes to serving in a way that seemed minor, and it led to a door you could not have imagined.
- You let go of something that looked secure, and in the empty space, a truer opportunity emerged.

From the outside, it just looks like life. From the inside, you begin to sense: *Light is leading me.*

When Light Leads You Through Shadow
It would be dishonest to talk about being led by Light and ignore the seasons that feel dark. There are times when prayers seem to bounce off the ceiling, the inner GPS goes quiet, or your former sense of clarity dissolves into fog.

This doesn't necessarily mean you've stepped out of God's will. Often, it means you are passing through a deeper part of it. A few truths for those seasons:

Silence is not absence. Sometimes the Teacher is quiet because you're already living the last thing you were given. Think of the cross. Jesus cries out, "My God, My God, why have You forsaken Me?". From the outside, it *looks* like abandonment. From the inside of that moment, it *feels* like abandonment.

Yet what happens next in the Gospel story? The veil of the temple is torn in two. The earth shakes. Graves open. A Roman centurion, of all people, looks up and says, "Truly this was the Son of God."

In the very moment when the Son feels most forsaken, heaven is not disengaged—it is *most deeply at work*, tearing down separation, unveiling access, revealing who He truly is. What looks and feels like silence and forsakenness on the surface is, at a deeper level, the precise moment of greatest union and redemption.

"Is it possible that some of the moments that feel most like 'God has left me' are actually the places where a deeper work is happening than I can see yet?"

Confusion can be mid-story, not final verdict. The disciples on Holy Saturday had no idea resurrection was coming. Their confusion was real, but it was not the end of the story.

Light often leads *through*, not around. The psalmist doesn't say, "You will never see a valley." He says, "Even though I walk through the valley of the shadow of death... You are with me."

In these seasons, being led by Light may look like:

- showing up for one more day,
- praying a very simple prayer: "Hold me,"
- letting others carry hope for you for a while,
- trusting that one day, you will look back and see a thread that is invisible right now.

"Instead of asking, 'Why is this happening?' what happens if I gently ask, 'How are You with me in this?'"

Being led by Light doesn't remove difficulty—it changes who you are inside it. Next, we widen the lens and learn to see as God sees.

* * *

Key Insight

Being led by Light is not about having advance notice of every turn; it is about learning to trust the Guide more than you fear the unknown. The inner GPS of Spirit does not hand you a finished map. It offers you a next step. As you follow:

- paths you never planned appear,
- detours are folded into deeper wisdom,
- delays become hidden preparation,
- and even your missteps are rerouted into grace.

The path of your life is not random. It is a conversation between your freedom and Divine Love...a story being co-written, step by surrendered step.

Reflection Practice
The Path That Forms Under Your Feet

Trace the Thread: Look back over the last 5–10 years. Where do you now see a "thread" of guidance—a pattern, a person, a moment—that you couldn't recognize then?

Releasing the Map: In what area of your life are you demanding a full map right now? Write a short prayer of release, something like: *"Light of the world, I release my demand to see the whole road. Show me the next faithful step, and give me courage to take it."*

Naming the Detour: Name one "detour" or "delay" you've resented. Ask gently: *"If I were to assume this is not wasted, what might it be forming in me?"* You can't change what happened, but you *can* change what you call it. Sometimes simply renaming something from "failure" to "formation," from "punishment" to "preparation," begins to change how your heart and nervous system relate to it. You don't need a clear answer—only a willingness to let the detour carry a new name, and with it, a new possibility

Listening to the Inner GPS: Set aside a few minutes in stillness. Place your hand over your heart and ask: *"If I trusted the inner GPS of Christ in me, where might it be quietly nudging me to move, to release, or to rest?"* Write down whatever arises, even if it seems small or ordinary.

Part IV: Love, Unity & the Divine Current

As you begin to see that your life is not just something you endure but a journey being quietly led by Light, another realization dawns:

- You are not walking alone, and you are not walking *against* the universe.
- You are being invited into the divine current itself...into a Life where seeing through the eyes of God, living from love as law, and awakening to your unity with the Source becomes not theory, but experience.

In the next part, we turn from the path beneath your feet to the Love that undergirds all paths; the Love in which you live, move, and have your being.

CHAPTER THIRTEEN

***

SEEING THROUGH THE EYES OF GOD

The God-Lens

If "God is love," then love is not just a nice spiritual add-on. Love is the governing principle of reality. Paul wrote that if you speak with the tongues of angels, fathom mysteries, move mountains with faith, giveaway everything you own, even your own body, but do not have love, you gain nothing. In other words:

- Power without *love* misses the point.
- Knowledge without *love* misses the point.
- Sacrifice without *love* misses the point.

Seeing through the eyes of God means you begin to measure things differently. You stop asking only, "Is this correct?" and start also asking, "Is this aligned with love?"

You begin to realize that a small act of kindness may be more in tune with God's heart than a perfectly argued doctrine delivered without compassion. A gentle apology may carry more divine weight than a hundred self-justifications.

You can be "right" and still be out of alignment with reality if your rightness is weaponized against people. Being honest with the truth means letting it read *you* before you ever try to use it on someone else. Truth that hasn't first softened your own heart will almost always harden someone else's.

"What if the real question behind every choice is not 'Is this impressive?' but 'Is this loving?'"

"I Want to Know God's Thoughts"

Physicist Albert Einstein once said, "I want to know God's thoughts; the rest are details." You don't have to solve relativity to feel that longing.

At the deepest level, every spiritual seeker—whether they use Bible language, mystical language, or no formal language at all—is saying something similar: "I want to see reality the way God sees it. I want to know what Love thinks about this situation, this person, this enemy, this wound, this world."

To see through the eyes of God is, in a very real way, to begin knowing "God's thoughts"—not in the sense of grasping all divine mysteries, but in the sense of sharing God's *way of looking.*

When you look at your own past through the eyes of God, shame loses its grip.

When you look at your enemies through the eyes of God, your hatred starts to crack.

When you look at your ordinary life through the eyes of God, nothing seems quite so "ordinary" anymore.

From the outside, nothing may change. From the inside, everything has.

The Spirit of Freedom

"Where the Spirit of the Lord is, there is freedom." Many of us heard that verse and subconsciously translated it as: "Where the Spirit of the Lord is, there are rules, anxiety about messing up, and low-grade guilt if you're enjoying anything too much."

But Scripture is clear: The atmosphere of God's Presence is *freedom,* not recklessness, not ego doing whatever it wants...freedom.

Freedom from the need to perform for love.

Freedom from the story that you are fundamentally unworthy.

Freedom from the compulsive need to compare, compete, or prove.

Freedom to be your true self in God, and to let others grow at their own pace.

Freedom to be the you God actually made, instead of the version you think everyone expects.

Seeing through the eyes of God means your inner posture toward yourself and others begins to loosen. You don't need to tighten around every flaw. You don't need to police every emotion. You don't need to hold people at a distance just because they're not where you are.

When Love is the lens, control can relax. You become a little less like a spiritual hall monitor, and a little more like a friend of the Bridegroom...happy just to see people move toward the Light, even if their steps look different from yours.

You'll begin to see how seriously your ego wants to be God's assistant manager. You can almost hear it say, "Don't worry, Lord, I'll handle the judging. You must be tired."

The Spirit smiles and replies, "You're free now. You can drop the clipboard."

"In my relationship with God and others, do I feel more like a beloved child in a spacious home, or an employee trying not to get fired?"

Seeing Others Through the God-Lens

If you let God's way of seeing touch your own self-image, it won't stay there. It will start spilling outward. You'll notice shifts like:

- From labels to stories. Instead of "That's just a lazy person," you begin to wonder, "What pain, fear, or story might be shaping this behavior?"
- From offense to curiosity. When someone wounds you, your first response might still be pain—but once you can breathe again, another question appears: *"What must they believe about themselves or the world to act this way?"*
- From writing people off to holding them in prayer. You may still set boundaries (and sometimes must), but you stop collapsing someone's entire identity into their worst moment.

This doesn't mean you become naive or boundary-less. God's love is not mushy; it is fierce and truthful. But even in correction, the eyes of God never lose sight of the person's true worth.

To see through the eyes of God is to see every person as made in the image of Love, warped in places by lies and wounds. And still held in the possibility of healing and homecoming.

You may not be able to trust everyone's choices. But you can learn to trust that no one is beyond the reach of the One who sees them.

"Who in my life have I been seeing only through the lens of their behavior; and what might it look like to ask, 'God, show me how You see them'?"

Seeing Yourself Through the God-Lens

Sometimes the hardest person to see through God's eyes is the one in the mirror. You may say all the right things about grace and identity, but deep down carry an inner script like:

- *"Yes, God is love... but I'm the exception."*
- *"Yes, there's forgiveness... but I'm on thin ice."*
- *"Yes, I'm a new creation, but He's mostly disappointed it's taking so long."*

To see yourself through the eyes of God is not to pretend you have no flaws. It is to finally stop agreeing with the lie that your flaws are the truest thing about you. It looks like:

- Letting passages like "beloved," "chosen," "new creation," "hidden with Christ in God" read *you*, not just decorate sermons.
- Allowing the Holy Spirit to contradict your harshest self-judgments.
- Treating your own heart as someone Christ thought worth dying for, not a project He regrets starting.

You won't wake up one day with all self-contempt gone. But over time, as you keep bringing your inner accusations into the Presence, you'll begin to notice; the voice of shame gets quieter, the voice of Love grows steadier, and the eyes you imagine looking at you start to soften.

When you see through the eyes of God, judgment softens and compassion rises. From there, the deeper truth comes into view: love isn't optional—it's the structure of reality.

What changes in your life if love is not merely a virtue, but the governing law?

* * *

Key Insight

Seeing through the eyes of God is not about escaping reality; it is about seeing reality from Love's side.

It means:

- Letting go of lenses shaped by fear, shame, and suspicion.
- Allowing yourself to be looked upon by a gaze that is truth *and* tenderness at once.
- Recognizing love as the governing principle of the universe, not just a moral suggestion.
- Learning to see yourself, others, and even your detours in the light of that Love.

You do not become less truthful when you see through the God-Lens. You become more truthful…because you finally include the deepest truth: God is love, and you, and they, and this world are held in that Love even when you cannot yet see how.

Reflection Practice: The God-Lens

God's Face Toward Me: Close your eyes for a moment and imagine God looking at you *right now.*

What expression do you instinctively see?

Where do you think that image came from—Scripture, upbringing, fear, someone else's wounds? Gently ask: *"Spirit of Truth, show me where this picture matches Your heart—and where it does not."*

Seeing Someone Differently: Think of one person who frustrates, hurts, or confuses you. In prayer, simply say: *"Holy One, show me how You see them."* Sit in silence for a minute or two. Notice any shift—a word, an image, a softening, a clearer boundary, a sense of their story. You don't have to force compassion; just allow a new angle to rise.

Reframing a Situation in Love: Choose one situation you've been viewing with anxiety or resentment. Ask: *"If Love had the first word here—not fear, not ego—how would this look different to me?"* Write a few sentences from the perspective of Love looking at that situation.

A Simple Prayer for the God-Lens: You might make this your quiet prayer for a week: *"God of Love, let me see as You see. Let my eyes be single, my heart be soft, and my judgments be replaced with Your truth and compassion. Let me see myself, others, and this world through Your eyes."*

CHAPTER FOURTEEN

* * *

LOVE AS LAW

The Only Law That Cannot Be Broken

By now, the pattern should be getting clear:

- awakening shows you there is more;
- alignment teaches you to walk with the Light;
- seeing through the eyes of God reveals that Love is the gaze behind everything real.

Chapter 14 is about the next startling realization, love is not just a *nice* idea, love is the *law* of reality. Paul says it bluntly: "And now these three remain: faith, hope, and love. But the greatest of these is love."

Not the most sentimental.

Not the most "optional."

The *greatest*.

You can think of it this way:

- Faith tunes your heart to trust.
- Hope anchors you in a future you cannot yet see.
- Love is the *substance* that faith and hope were reaching for all along.

If God is love, then love is not just one value among many in competition. Love is the governing reality-the very structure of the universe itself.

"What if love is not just what God prefers—but the way the universe actually works at its deepest level?"

Love as the Law of Reality

The perfect law of liberty is the law by which you become most free when you're most aligned with love. Think of how other laws operate:

Gravity doesn't punish you. It simply describes how mass and space relate.

Fire doesn't hate you if you touch it. It does what fire does.

In the same way, love is not an arbitrary moral rule God made up. Love describes how life in God actually functions. When you move in love, you move with reality. When you move against love, you feel friction—inside and out.

This is why Jesus boils the entire law and prophets down to two commands:

Love God with all your heart, soul, mind, and strength.
Love your neighbor as yourself.

Then He says something even more radical: "On these two commandments hang all the Law and the Prophets."

Everything else is commentary.

"If love is the law everything else hangs on, where have I been majoring in the minors?"

Truth and Love: Two Names for One Reality

It's often said that *truth and love are synonymous.* We're used to treating them like opposites:

- "I'm not trying to be loving; I'm just telling the truth."
- "I didn't tell them the truth; I wanted to be loving."

But in God, truth and love never pull against each other. If what you're saying is genuinely true, it will be rooted in love. If what you're calling "love" requires you to abandon truth, it's just fear in a softer outfit.

You know you've lost the God-Lens when "truth" feels like a hammer and "love" feels like enabling. Through the eyes of God:

- Truth reveals what is real because love wants to heal it.
- Love moves toward what is real because truth can finally set it free.

You don't have to choose between being honest and being kind. You're invited to become the kind of person for whom honesty itself becomes an act of kindness.

Forgiveness as Liberation (Not Amnesia)

If love is the law, forgiveness is one of its sharpest tools. Jesus ties forgiveness directly to the way reality works: "Forgive, and you will be forgiven...with the measure you use, it will be measured to you."

Forgiveness is not:

- saying what happened was okay,
- pretending it didn't hurt,
- reconciling with someone who's unsafe,
- or losing all boundaries and calling it "grace."

Forgiveness is:

- releasing your right to hold the other person's soul hostage,
- handing the case over to a higher court,
- letting yourself step out of the prison you built for them and accidentally locked yourself inside.

Unforgiveness feels powerful in the moment: "I will never let this go. I will *remember* what you did." But neurologically, chronic resentment keeps your nervous system on high alert. Your body re-lives the injury every time you rehearse the story. Stress hormones remain elevated. Muscles stay braced. The past keeps borrowing energy from the present.

Science is just putting numbers on what Jesus already said:

> *People who cultivate forgiveness tend to have lower blood pressure, less chronic stress, and greater emotional resilience.*

Forgiveness is not just "spiritual." It's how your entire being was designed to move back into alignment with love. It is truly one of the greatest gifts you can give someone.

"Who is actually living inside the prison cell—me, or the person I refuse to forgive?"

"People Are Easy to Love... Until They're Not"

Let's be honest. Loving sunsets, puppies, and people who agree with you is easy. Loving the driver who cuts you off, the coworker who undermines you, or the family member whose every text raises your blood pressure; that's where love stops being an idea and becomes a *practice*.

People are easy to love... until they're not.

That gap, in between "They're wonderful" and "I can't stand them", is where the law of love is forged into muscle. Love as law doesn't mean: you feel warm feelings toward everyone all the time, you enjoy being mistreated, or you pretend unhealthy dynamics are fine.

It means that even when someone's behavior requires boundaries, consequences, or distance, you still refuse to dehumanize them in your heart. You can say, "No" to abuse, "Stop" to manipulation, and "This can't continue" to certain patterns, while still saying "Yes" to seeing that person as more than their worst moment.

Love is not weak. It is the strongest thing in the universe. It can say, "I release you," even when every cell wants to stay angry.

The Science of Compassion (Why Love Changes Your Brain)

Compassion isn't just "being nice." It literally reshapes your brain. Studies on compassion meditation and loving-kindness prayer have shown:

- increased activity in regions of the brain related to empathy and emotional regulation,
- decreased reactivity in fear and threat centers,
- greater capacity to hold others' pain without being overwhelmed.

On the physiological side, when you intentionally practice forgiveness or compassion:

- your heart rhythm often becomes more coherent,

- your stress hormones decrease,
- your body shifts from fight-or-flight into a state more conducive to healing.

In other words…when Jesus calls you to love your enemies, He is not asking you to violate your design. He is inviting you *into* the way you were designed to function at your healthiest.

Love is not only the law of heaven. It is the law that your own nervous system recognizes as home.

"What would it mean to treat love not as extra credit, but as the baseline my brain and body were actually built for?"

Choosing Love on Purpose (When You Don't Feel Like It)

Love as law does not mean love as automatic. If that were the case, we wouldn't need Jesus to tell us to do it. Most of the time, love is a choice *before* it is a feeling.

Here's a simple framework for choosing love on purpose in difficult moments:

Pause the Script: When you're triggered, your brain starts running its usual story: "They always do this." "I have to defend myself." "I'll show them."

One deep breath is often enough to interrupt the script. Whisper inwardly: *"This is a holy moment. I get to choose who I am here."*

Remember Who's in Front of You: Instead of seeing "the rude cashier," remember: a whole life stands in front of you…with history, with wounds, with fears, with a heart God loves. You don't have to know their story. You just have to refuse to reduce them to this one behavior.

Ask: "What Would Love Do That Fear Never Thinks Of?" Fear asks: "How do I win this?", "How do I protect my ego?" Love asks: "What response here is most aligned with truth *and* kindness?", "What would I hope someone would do for me if I were having my worst day?"

- *Sometimes love will smile.*
- *Sometimes love will be silent.*

- *Sometimes love will name a boundary.*

Take the Smallest Loving Step: You don't have to fix the relationship. You don't have to feel *ready*. Just take one small step in the direction of love:

- A softer tone.
- A slower reply.
- A refusal to send the angry text.
- A genuine, "Help me understand what you meant." Love grows in inches, not miles.

Let God Love Through You: When you reach the end of your own capacity, you can pray: "Love, love them through me. I don't have it in me right now but I offer You my willingness."

Love as law is not love as self-strain. It is love as cooperation with the One who *is* love. Love is not sentiment—it is alignment with the deepest truth. And when love becomes your root, your life begins to unify.

"In the last conflict I had, where could one small loving step have changed the entire tone?"

Choose one relationship today and bring one act of clean love into it...no scoreboard, no rehearsal.

* * *

Key Insight

Love is not a suggestion, an accessory, or an optional personality trait. Love is the law of life in God. To live in love is to live in alignment with reality. To move against love is to suffer the friction of resisting what you were made for.

Truth without love warps.

Power without love wounds.

Faith without love misfires.

But even the smallest act of love—a forgiving word, a patient pause, a boundary set without hatred—moves your life into the current of how things actually are in God.

Love is the only law that cannot be broken. You can ignore it, resist it, or delay it—but in the end, it is Love that remains.

Reflection Practice
<u>Choosing Love on Purpose</u>

Where Have I Been "Right" Without Love?: Think of a recent situation where you knew you were correct—but your correctness left someone feeling small or unseen. Ask gently: *"What would it have looked like to be just as honest, but more loving?"*

A Forgiveness You've Delayed: Bring one person to mind whom you struggle to forgive. You don't have to force a feeling. Pray simply:

"I don't know how to forgive them, but I'm willing to be made willing. Show me what freedom would look like here."

A 24-Hour Love Experiment: For one day, set the quiet intention: "Today, I will choose the smallest loving response I can see in each interaction." At night, review: How did it feel? What surprised you? What was hardest?

Prayer for Living the Law of Love: You might whisper this as a daily grounding:

> "God of Love, reveal Your law in my heart. Let love be the measure of my words, the source of my actions, and the lens of my seeing. Where I've made the details bigger than Your heart, bring me back to the One thing that never fails: love."

CHAPTER FIFTEEN

***

THE UNIFIED LIFE

Living as One in the One

There is a particular kind of exhaustion that has nothing to do with how much you slept. It's the tiredness of feeling like more than one person at the same time.

One self that trusts God and another that secretly panics. One self that talks about grace and another that quietly believes it doesn't apply to you. One self that shows up in "spiritual moments" and another that just tries to survive "real life."

Most of us don't wake up thinking, "Today, I'd like to be wildly inconsistent with my deepest self." And yet, if we pay attention, there's often a quiet split running through our days.

Underneath all our seeking, striving, and self-improvement, there is a simpler longing many of us barely know how to name:

I just want to feel together inside.

I don't just want to visit wholeness on good days.

I want to live from it.

This isn't just your private wish. It is at the very center of Jesus' heart for you.

On the night before His death, with the weight of the world pressing in, Jesus prayed one of the most intimate prayers we have on record. He did not ask the Father to make us more impressive, more productive, or more correct. He asked for something far deeper:

"That they may all be one; as You, Father, are in Me, and I in You, that they also may be in Us."

Oneness is not a bonus level for advanced souls. It is the desire of Christ Himself, that we would share in the same kind of unbroken communion He has with the Father.

The problem is, most of us don't feel like walking pictures of oneness. We feel:

- split between faith and fear,
- split between "religious or church self" and "work self,"
- split between what we say we believe and how we actually live on Tuesday afternoon.

No wonder we're tired. Living as two is exhausting.

This chapter is about that gap. It's about what happens when the Spirit begins to heal the inner divide, so that the life you live on the outside and the life God sees on the inside slowly begin to tell the same story.

You could call it the unified life; not a life without flaws or questions, but a life where your body, mind, and spirit, your "spiritual self" and your "ordinary self," are being gathered into one real, honest, God-held you.

In other words, the you that prays for world peace and the you that loses patience in traffic are finally learning to sit at the same table.

"What if wholeness, union with God, is not a reward waiting at the end of the journey, but the truth I'm slowly waking up to right now?"

You Were Born From Union, Not Separation

The story many of us absorbed goes something like this:

- You were born separated from God.
- Life proved how disappointingly true that was.
- If you do this right, maybe one day you'll finally be close.

But Scripture whispers a better story:

- You were created *in* God's image.
- You live and move and have your being *in* God.

Christ is described as "the true Light that gives light to everyone."

Grace is not God reluctantly bridging a distance He secretly prefers. Grace is God revealing a union that fear and blindness made you *feel* cut off from. Sin, lies, trauma, and confusion are real. They matter. They wound. They distort. But they do not have the power to rewrite your origin story.

Before you were hurt, you were held.
Before you were confused, you were known.
Before you were labeled, you were loved.

The unified life is not about climbing into God. It's about letting the Spirit peel away everything that says you were ever outside. It's like all the rooms in your inner house finally being connected—no locked closets, no "off-limits" parts of you that God isn't allowed to touch.

Childhood Identity vs. Spiritual Identity

Early on, we learn who we are by what people mirror back to us. Maybe you grew up hearing:

- "You're the responsible one."
- "You're the shy one."
- "You're the difficult one."
- "You're the smart one."
- "You're the one who always messes things up."

If you were *really* lucky (sarcasm intended), you got to be: the golden child on Monday, the disappointment on Tuesday, and the invisible one by Thursday.

The ego takes notes. It builds an identity around these mirrors: "I am what I achieve." "I am what people think of me." "I am the one who must hold everything together." "I am the one who always drops the ball."

We carry those stories into adulthood like name tags no one asked us to keep wearing. Then spiritual language enters:

- "Beloved."
- "New creation."
- "Temple of the Holy Spirit."
- "In Christ."

And somewhere inside, a quiet argument begins: "Am I the anxious, approval-hungry kid who never felt enough...or this beloved child of God I keep hearing about?"

The unified life is what happens when those two no longer live as enemies; when the wounded child is gently gathered into the arms of the deeper identity that was always true.

You don't have to fight your history. You let your history be re-read in the light of who you are in God.

"What labels from childhood am I still wearing—and what name does Love call me instead?"

"That They May Be One": Oneness Without Sameness

When Jesus prays, "That they may be one," He doesn't mean that everyone will look, think, and vote exactly the same, that individuality is erased, or that healthy boundaries evaporate into a spiritual group hug.

Oneness is not sameness. It is harmony. Think:

- many notes, one song;
- many cells, one body;
- many branches, one Vine.

A painter doesn't insist every color on the canvas be the same shade of blue, just to keep it simple. *The beauty is in the contrast.* Unity doesn't erase difference; it weaves difference into a meaningful whole.

In the same way, the unified life is not you dissolving into a bland spiritual fog. It is you becoming most fully yourself in God, while recognizing you are not, and never were, separate from the rest of the family.

True unity honors real difference. Forced sameness is not unity; it's distortion.

You are a unique expression of the One Life. Not the only expression. If God wanted a world full of your exact personality, He would've stopped after you. The fact that He didn't is both humbling and a relief.

A Nervous System Built for Oneness (Science Corner)

All this talk about oneness might sound mystical, but your biology quietly nods along. When people experience deep connection, compassion, heartfelt prayer, or a sense of unity with God and others, their brain and body respond.

Research on contemplative practices and nondual awareness shows things like:

- Quieter self-referential chatter. Areas of the brain involved in obsessive self-focus can calm down, making room for a more spacious sense of "I" that includes others.
- Increased empathy and compassion. Networks linked to understanding others' feelings become more active and integrated.
- Improved heart–brain coherence. When people rest in gratitude, love, or connection, their nervous system organizes into smoother, more ordered patterns.

In simple terms:

- When you live as if you are separate and threatened, your body stays braced.
- When you live as if you belong; to God, to others, to this moment, your body remembers how to rest.

Your nervous system isn't offended by oneness. It's *relieved*. The unified life is not just a theological upgrade; it's your whole being returning to its native setting: connected.

"Where in my life does my body already know I'm safe and connected, and how might that be a hint of a deeper spiritual truth?"

Signs You Are Living a More Unified Life

You will not wake up one day with a trumpet blast and a certificate that says, "Congratulations, you are now perfectly unified." But there *are* gentle signs:

Less Inner Civil War: You still have conflicting thoughts, but you are less interested in attacking yourself for them. You begin saying things like: "Part of me is scared; part of me wants to trust. Both can sit here with God." The war softens into a conversation.

Fewer Compartments: "Soul time" and "real life" start merging. You find yourself praying while doing dishes. You feel God's presence in the carpool line. Scripture comes to mind during staff meetings, not just during "quiet time."

Life stops feeling like two different worlds. It becomes one continuous field where Love keeps showing up.

Less Need to Perform for God: Your prayers sound less like performance reviews and more like actual conversations. • "Here's who I really am today." • "Here's what I actually feel." • "Here's where I'm tired and over it."

Instead of bracing for punishment, you expect Presence.

Freedom to Let Others Be in Process: As the split within you heals, you become less threatened by the splits in others. You can say: "They're not there yet—and that's okay. Neither am I." You don't have to micromanage everyone's journey.

You can trust the same Love working in you to be working in them.

No More "Spiritual Mode" vs. "Real Life Mode"
Many of us were trained to live like this:

Spiritual mode: church, worship music, small group, "language upgrade" ("Brother, I'm just so blessed").

Real life mode: emails, bills, arguments, Netflix, mild road rage.

The unified life gently laughs at that split. Jesus didn't clock in and out of "ministry mode." He didn't heal from 9–5, then spend evenings glaring at fishermen and scrolling GalileeTok.

He moved through weddings, long walks, meals, storms, tears, and silence with the same inner union:
> *"I and the Father are one."*
> *"The Father is in Me and I am in the Father."*

You are invited into that same awareness...not as doctrine only, but as lived reality: "Christ in you, the hope of glory."

The unified life is what happens when there is no longer a "place" where God is *not*:

- Not in the office.
- Not at the grocery store.
- Not in traffic.
- Not in grief.
- Not in laughter.

Everywhere you go... One Life. One Presence, expressing through ten thousand ordinary moments.

"Where do I still unconsciously act as if God steps out for a smoke break and leaves me on my own?"

Practice Box—The Breath of Oneness
The Breath of Oneness
Use this simple practice whenever you feel fragmented, alone, or pulled in a hundred directions.

Pause and Place a Hand on Your Heart: You don't have to "feel spiritual." Just stop for a moment and notice that you are here.

Inhale: "In You I live..." As you breathe in, quietly say: "In You I live..." Imagine your breath as a reminder that your whole being is held in God.

Exhale: "...and move and have my being." As you breathe out, say: "...and move and have my being." Let your exhale be a release of the illusion that you are separate, on your own.

Include Your Whole Self: On the next breath, gently bring to mind:

- your thoughts
- your emotions
- your body
- your story so far

Whisper: "All of me, in You."

Include Others: Now call to mind someone close to you, then someone difficult, then your wider community. With each, simply breathe and say: "You in them, them in You."

Rest in Silence: Sit for 30 seconds to a few minutes with no agenda. Let your breath move. Let your shoulders drop. You're not trying to *achieve* oneness; you're allowing yourself to feel what has always been true.

Even a short version; one or two breaths in the middle of your day can help your mind and body remember:

I am not two.
I am one person, held in One Love.

A unified life is the fruit of living from what is real. Now we turn our attention toward what comes next—beginning with a brief map of Christian views on the life beyond.

* * *

Key Insight

The unified life is not spiritual perfection; it is spiritual integration. It is the slow, grace-filled process of:

- letting your many inner "selves" be gathered into one story in God,
- allowing your childhood labels to be renamed in the light of who you truly are,
- living one life instead of juggling five different personas,
- and discovering that you were never as separate from God, or from others, as fear and shame led you to believe.

You are not trying to glue yourself together from the outside. You are awakening to the One in whom you have been held all along.

Reflection Practice

Living the Unified Life

Spot the Compartments: Finish these sentences honestly: "I feel close to God when ___, but far from God when ___." "I'm my 'spiritual self' when ___, but my 'regular self' when ___." Notice where you still live in two worlds.

Rename a Label: Write down one old identity label you've carried (e.g., "the failure," "the strong one," "the problem," "the fixer").

Then ask: *"What does Love call me instead?"* Sit with it. Let a new word rise: "Beloved," "Held," "Learning," "Brave," "Growing."

A Day Without Switching Masks: Choose one day to practice this intention: "Today, I will be the same 'me' in every setting; honest, present, and aware of God with me." You don't have to overshare; just notice when you feel tempted to perform or hide and gently return to authenticity.

Prayer for Wholeness: You might pray this at night or upon waking:

"Spirit of Oneness, I am tired of living divided. Gather my thoughts, my emotions, my body, and my story into one true life in You. Let there be no corner of my being where Your love is not welcome. Make me whole, inside and out, not by erasing who I am, but by revealing who I have always been in You."

PART V: REALIZATION & THE ETERNAL JOURNEY

The Soul's Continuation in Light

The chapters that follow may feel more controversial than what we've explored so far, depending on your background and beliefs.

My aim is not to argue or divide, but to keep us rooted in the One constant we share: unconditional love. Even if we don't see every detail the same way, we can still walk together in that Love. So I invite you to stay at the table with me as we move through these next chapters.

If union is the deepest truth now, then death is not the end of that union, it is its continuation in another form. We move from a unified life here into a unified life that never ends, in the Light that has always been our home.

Most of this book focuses on awakening *here*...learning to live as Light, as love, as union, in the middle of ordinary human days. But eventually, a deeper question rises: *If union is real now... what happens when this life ends?*

For many, the topic of death has been wrapped in fear: threats of punishment, visions of endless torment, or the quiet suspicion that this one fragile lifetime is your only chance. And if you don't get it right, you're finished.

Yet everything we've explored so far points in another direction:

- A God who is Love, not cruelty.
- A universe shaped by law-like compassion and coherence.
- A soul made for oneness, not abandonment.

If you are held in Love now, that Love does not drop you at the threshold of death.

Part V is about realization in its fullest sense: not just realizing the Light *within* this life, but discovering that this life is only one chapter in an eternal story. In these chapters we will explore:

- What happens when we die: transition, Presence, and the first moments beyond the body.
- The life review: not as courtroom drama, but as luminous clarity, seeing your life through the eyes of Love.
- Divine justice: not retribution, but revelation and restoration; what "lake of fire," consequence, and "what you bind on earth" mean from differing perspectives.
- Eternal growth: what it means that "of His kingdom there will be no end," and why awakening is the beginning, not the finish line.

This is not a blueprint of heaven or a spiritual sightseeing guide. It is an invitation to view death in the same Light that has been reframing your understanding of life.

Not as separation, -> but as continuation.

Not as exile, -> but as passage.

Not as God finally revealing how disappointed He was, -> but as God revealing how thoroughly He has always loved.

CHAPTER SIXTEEN

*** * ***

A Brief Map of Christian Views on What Comes Next

Christians who love Jesus and take Scripture seriously have disagreed for centuries about what happens when we die. Some picture eternal separation, some believe in eventual restoration, some see death as a sleep until resurrection, and many live somewhere in the questions between. Good, sincere, Bible-loving people land in different places.

This chapter is not here to settle the debate or hand you a new label. It's simply a brief map; a way of saying, *you're not crazy for asking these questions. You're not the first to wrestle with them.* Followers of Christ have read the same Bible and, with prayer and humility, have come to different conclusions about the "second death," the great white throne judgment, and the final shape of eternity.

My aim is not to argue, but to name a few of the main views so that as we move forward, you know I'm not pretending there is only one way Christians have ever seen this.

Traditional View: Eternal Conscious Punishment: In the traditional view, sometimes called eternal conscious punishment, those who finally reject God face an eternity of conscious separation from His presence. Judgment is real, final, and everlasting. The imagery of the great white throne judgment in Revelation 20 is often central here: the dead are raised, books are opened, each person is judged according to what they have done, and "anyone whose name was not found written in the book of life" is thrown into "the lake of fire." This lake of fire is described as "the second death", a phrase that, in this view, points not to annihilation, but to a final, irreversible state of separation and suffering.

Those who hold this view take very seriously Jesus' warnings about "eternal punishment" (Matthew 25:46), the imagery of undying worm and unquenchable fire (Mark 9:48), and the description of torment that "has no rest day or night" (Revelation 14:11). They emphasize that God is not only love, but also holy and just, and that our choices in this life carry real, eternal weight. For many, this view protects the seriousness of sin and the urgency of repentance.

At the same time, it raises deep questions for others: How do we hold together the picture of a God who is love with the idea of endless, conscious torment? What does it mean for God to be "all in all" if a portion of His creation is eternally lost? People who wrestle with these questions are not always trying to escape the Bible; often, they are trying to listen to the whole of Scripture and the Spirit's witness to the character of God.

Conditional Immortality / Annihilationism: Another view, often called conditional immortality or annihilationism, agrees that judgment is real and serious, but understands the "second death" more literally. In this view, human beings are not inherently immortal. Eternal life is a gift given in Christ, not a default setting of the soul. Those who ultimately refuse God's grace are judged, and their end is not eternal, conscious torment, but final destruction...a ceasing to exist.

Here, the language of "the wages of sin is death" (Romans 6:23), "fear Him who can destroy both soul and body in hell" (Matthew 10:28), and "everlasting destruction" (2 Thessalonians 1:9) is read as pointing to genuine, irreversible loss of life rather than eternal suffering. The lake of fire and second death in Revelation 20 are seen as images of ultimate extinction; the final undoing of everything in us that has chosen against God. The great white throne judgment is still sober and terrifying, but its outcome is destruction, not everlasting torment.

Those who hold this view often do so because they want to take seriously both the reality of judgment and the goodness of God. They feel this understanding better fits the biblical emphasis on life versus death, perishing versus eternal life, and avoids the moral difficulty of infinite conscious torment. Critics of this view worry that it may soften the warnings of Scripture or reduce the felt urgency of turning to God. Again, sincere believers stand on both sides of that concern.

Universal Reconciliation / Hopeful Universalism: A third view, often called universal reconciliation, ultimate reconciliation, or hopeful universalism, believes that God's judgment is real, but ultimately restorative rather than purely retributive. In this understanding, the images of fire; whether "lake of fire," "unquenchable fire," or "everyone will be salted with fire", are seen as purifying rather than merely punitive. The second death can be understood as the death of the false self, the egoic, fear-based identity that cannot inherit the kingdom of God, rather than the final destruction of the person God loves.

Those who lean this way look closely at passages that speak of all things being reconciled (Colossians 1:19–20), of God being "all in all" (1 Corinthians 15:28), of "as in Adam all die, so in Christ all will be made alive" (1 Corinthians 15:22), and of every knee bowing and every tongue confessing that Jesus Christ is Lord (Philippians 2:10–11). They see the great white throne judgment as utterly real, but ultimately ordered toward healing, revelation, and restoration; the burning away of what cannot remain, until what is left is the true self in Christ.

In this view, even if there is a long and painful journey for some beyond this life, God's love and patience do not end at the grave. Divine justice is not set against mercy; it is one more expression of mercy. Critics of this view worry that it may undercut the seriousness of sin or suggest that our choices don't really matter if everyone is "fine in the end." Those who hold it insist that choices *do* matter deeply, that judgment is *real* and *severe*, but that God's desire and ability to redeem is even deeper still.

Trustful Agnosticism: There is also what we might call trustful agnosticism, not agnostic about God, but agnostic about the exact mechanics of the afterlife. People in this space affirm what Scripture clearly teaches: that there will be a judgment, that our lives will be brought into the Light, that there is both warning and promise, that there is resurrection, and that God will set the world right. But they are cautious about drawing detailed charts of who ends up where and how.

They might say something like: *"I know that God is just, God is merciful, God is love, and God is wiser than I am. I know that Jesus will judge in perfect truth. I don't know exactly how that will look for every soul, and I don't want to pretend I do."* They take seriously passages that speak of mystery; "we see in part," "we know in part," "how unsearchable His judgments", and are content to leave more in God's hands than in their diagrams.

This posture can be frustrating if we want certainty and clean lines. But it can also be a humble and honest way of living with the tension Scripture itself holds: strong warnings, strong promises, and a God whose ways are higher than ours. Trustful agnosticism doesn't mean "anything goes"; it means "God knows, and I trust His heart more than my charts."

Heaven and Hell as Present Reality: There is another way some followers of Jesus talk about heaven and hell; not as only future locations, but as present realities we begin to experience here and now. This view doesn't always replace the others; often it sits alongside them. Someone might still believe in a final judgment and a life beyond death, while also insisting that heaven and hell are, in a very real sense, already at work in the human heart.

From this perspective, heaven is not just a distant place where we go later, but the lived experience of union with God; of love, peace, joy, and alignment with the Light. Hell is not just a future pit, but the inner reality of separation, shame, hatred, or self-will turned in on itself. When Jesus talks about the kingdom of God being "at hand," or "within you," people in this stream hear an invitation to wake up to a reality that has already begun.

They might say: *Whenever you live in love, forgiveness, and Presence, you are already tasting heaven. Whenever you cling to bitterness, violence, or deception, you are tasting hell.* The fire imagery in Scripture, the burning away of what cannot last, the refining of gold, can be seen as something that begins even now, as the Spirit brings our inner life into the Light.

In this view, the great white throne judgment and the second death can still be real future events, but they are also the full unveiling of what has been forming inside us all along. Judgment doesn't come out of nowhere; it reveals what we have been agreeing with in this life: love or fear, truth or illusion, union or resistance.

The strength of this approach is that it refuses to let questions about "later" distract us from the urgency of now. It reminds us that eternity isn't just about where we go when we die; it's about the kind of person we are becoming in each moment. Critics sometimes worry that this emphasis could downplay the reality of final judgment or make heaven and hell seem purely psychological. But at its best, this view calls us to take seriously the spiritual atmosphere we are cultivating right now...because whatever comes after death will not be disconnected from the life we are living in *this moment*.

Why Name These Views at All?

You may find yourself clearly in one of these camps. You may find pieces of yourself in two or three of them. You may still be searching. Wherever you are, you are not alone. My purpose in this book is not to recruit you into a particular system, but to keep our attention on the character of God as revealed in Jesus: God as Love, God as Light, God as the One who never stops reaching, never stops inviting, never stops telling the truth about us in a way that heals rather than destroys.

When we speak later about near-death experiences, the life review, divine justice, and eternal growth, I want you to know that I see this spectrum. I am not pretending everybody agrees. I am also not asking you to throw away what you have sincerely come to believe. I am simply asking you to hold one question open as we walk through Part V together:

If God is as loving, truthful, and persistent as Jesus reveals; if union with Him is the deepest reality now, then what would it mean for death, judgment, and "what comes next" to be consistent with that same heart?

We may not all land in the exact same place on the charts. But if we can stay at the table with that question, rooted in Love, then even our differences can become part of how the Light keeps widening our view.

You don't have to resolve every question about the afterlife to walk in the Light that's in front of you. This chapter can be a map in your hand...not so you can control the journey, but so you can keep trusting the Guide. Naming viewpoints isn't the goal, seeking truth with humility is. So now we turn from the map to the mystery itself: what happens when we die?

* * *

KEY INSIGHTS

Sincere Christians read the same Bible and land in different places. Eternal conscious punishment, conditional immortality, universal reconciliation, "I don't know but I trust God," and "heaven/hell as present realities" are not inventions of people who don't care about Scripture, they're attempts to be faithful to it.

Every view is trying to protect something important. Some are guarding the seriousness of sin and judgment. Some are guarding the goodness and character of God. Some are guarding humility in the face of mystery. Behind every position is a picture of who God is.

"Second death," "lake of fire," and judgment are real themes, not decorations. Scripture does not treat our choices as trivial. Whatever we believe about the details, there is a real unveiling of the heart, a real encounter with Truth, and real consequence for what we cling to.

Heaven and hell are not only "later"; they begin now. Union, love, peace, bitterness, hatred, and separation are already being tasted in our inner world. Eternity is not disconnected from the kind of person we are becoming in this moment.

We see in part. God does not. Charts differ. Systems differ. What does not change is the character of God revealed in Jesus: Love, Light, Truth, and a relentless desire to heal and restore. Whatever lies beyond the doorway of death will not contradict that Heart.

REFLECTION PRACTICE

Take a few quiet minutes with a journal or just a deep, honest inner conversation with God. Name your current leaning. Gently, without analysis, which view (or combination) do you instinctively lean toward right now:

- Traditional eternal separation?
- Annihilation/conditional immortality?
- Universal reconciliation/hope?
- "I don't know, but I trust God"?
- Heaven/hell as present realities?

Write it in a simple sentence: "Right now, I mostly lean toward _____."

Notice what you're protecting. Ask yourself: *What am I most trying to protect with this view?*

- God's justice?
- God's love?
- The seriousness of sin?
- The reality of consequences?
- My fear? My hope? My need for certainty?

Let the answer surface without judgment.

Bring that into the Light. In your own words, pray something like:

"God, this is how I see things right now. This is what I'm trying to protect. If my view is too small, too harsh, too soft, or too limited, please widen it. Let my picture of what comes next be shaped more by Your heart than by my fear or my need to be right."

Return to the one thing you know. Sit for a moment with a single, anchoring truth. For example:

- "God is love."
- "God is just and merciful."
- "Jesus is the exact image of God's heart."
- "Nothing can separate us from the love of God."

Breathe that truth in slowly. Let it sink below the arguments into your actual being.

Live today in light of that truth. Ask: "If this one truth is real, how would it change the way I live *today*; the way I speak, forgive, listen, or love?"

Let the mystery of "then" deepen your faithfulness now, instead of paralyzing you.

CHAPTER SEVENTEEN

***

WHAT HAPPENS WHEN WE DIE

Crossing the Threshold of Light

No matter what we believe, one statistic remains stubbornly universal...100% of us will die. We can eat clean, exercise, meditate, take vitamins, bio-hack our sleep, and stretch this life as far as grace and genetics allow. But eventually, every one of us will be asked to do the same unthinkable thing:

- Let go.
- Let go of the body.
- Let go of the roles.
- Let go of the calendar, the to-do list, the careful identity we spent decades building.

Even if you're a person of faith, the question still hums beneath the surface:

What actually happens when I die?

Many of us were handed answers: some comforting, some terrifying, some so vague they might as well have been a shrug. For some, death was presented in a threatening tone: *"If you died tonight, do you know where you'd go?"*

Yet if everything we've explored in this book is true, if God is love, if Christ is Light, if union is the deepest reality, then wouldn't whatever happens when we die be consistent with that character?

If God has been patient with us here, why imagine Him impatient there? If He has been a relentless pursuer of the heart in this life, why assume He becomes distant or indifferent in the next?
If every breath we've taken has been held inside a Love that will not let us go, why picture death as falling out of those hands instead of deeper into them?

I am not claiming to know the mechanics of heaven or the exact details of what comes next. But I trust the continuity of God's character. Whatever the contours of the next realm may be, they will not contradict the One who is love, who is Light, who has already woven Himself into every breath and every moment of our existence.

Whatever death is, it will not be a break in the story of God's love...it will be a chapter written in the same handwriting. God does not stop being God at the edge of your final breath.

"If Love has held me in every moment I've been aware of... could it really abandon me in the one moment I need it most?"

Death as a Threshold, Not a Disappearance

We often talk about death as if it were a vanishing: "He's gone.", "She's no longer with us." From the side of those still in bodies, that's how it feels.

But even basic physics hints at something deeper: Energy cannot be destroyed. It can change form, but it does not cease to exist.

Your body returns to the elements. Your breath returns to the air. But your "you-ness", your consciousness, your soul, the life of God in you, does not evaporate.

In the language of faith, to be "absent from the body" is to be "present with the Lord." Not drifted into nowhere...Present. Awakening here prepares you for that awareness there.

Think of this life as a room with the lights turned down low. You learn to recognize God's presence in whispers:

- a sense of peace in prayer,
- a conviction of truth,
- a joy that makes no sense on paper,

- a love that catches you off guard.

Death is not God walking into the room. God has been there the whole time. Death is the lights coming fully on. The One you met in glimpses, you now meet without obstruction. The Presence you trusted by faith, you now encounter by direct knowing.

Near-Death Experiences: Fear, Discernment, and the Light

For some readers, the moment I mention near-death experiences, alarm bells start ringing. I understand that. Many of us were warned that anything involving tunnels of light, leaving the body, or seeing departed loved ones must be demonic deception. We were told that God stopped speaking that way, that the Bible is all we need, and that anything beyond that is at best imagination and at worst the enemy in disguise.

Why do some Christians see NDEs as dangerous or demonic? Because they're rightly concerned about deception. Because not every spiritual experience is from God. Because some NDE accounts seem to contradict their theology or raise questions they don't know how to answer. And when we're afraid of being misled, the safest response can feel like rejecting all of it.

But if we slow down and look more carefully, a different picture begins to emerge. The consistent fruit of most near-death testimonies is not rebellion, pride, or obsession with darkness; it's repentance, humility, overflowing love for God and people, loss of the fear of death, and a deeper desire to live a life of integrity.

People who were self-absorbed often come back radically more compassionate. Those who were terrified of God often return speaking of a Presence of overwhelming love and truth that exposed everything yet condemned nothing. That doesn't sound like the work of a liar whose goal is to steal, kill, and destroy.

Across thousands of these stories, one thread appears again and again: a radiant Presence of Love and Light that is not just *seen* but somehow *entered into*. Many experiencers say the Light didn't only surround them, it seemed to move through them, to become part of them, as if they were made of the same love they were meeting. They often struggle to describe it, but the impact is unmistakable: they come back different, carrying some of that Light with them into ordinary life.

That doesn't mean we build an entire theology on NDEs or treat every detail as infallible. We don't. Experience, ours or anyone else's, must always be held up to the Light and tested.

But it may mean we begin to treat these stories less like forbidden territory and more like modern-day parables: imperfect human language pointing toward a larger reality, often lining up with what Jesus and Scripture have been saying all along about God's character.

With that in mind, we can listen without fear, with discernment and an open heart.

Near-death testimonies from around the world, across cultures and ages, tend to describe the moment of dying in surprisingly similar ways.

While every story is unique, many include things like:
- a sense of leaving the body and seeing it from above,
- a feeling of peace far greater than anything known on earth,
- the strange realization, "I am still *me*, even though that body down there is not moving."

One person described it this way: "It was like stepping out of a tight shoe I didn't know was hurting." The body releases. The nervous system goes quiet. But awareness does not blink out. It opens.

You are not less conscious -> you are more conscious. You are not less alive -> you are more alive.

The physical senses fall away, and yet what you *are*; your spirit, your deepest Self in God, remains clear. And almost universally, those who've been near this threshold say the same thing: "The fear was gone."

The fear of death belongs mostly to those who are still trying not to die. Once the crossing begins, those who have glimpsed it often describe a peace that feels like finally remembering something you always knew, but had forgotten.

Being Met by Presence

From there, something else tends to happen: You are not left alone. In countless testimonies, people speak of being met:

- by a radiant Being of Light,
- by Jesus,
- by angels,
- by beloved family members who have already passed,
- by a Presence that can only be described as unconditional love and total knowing.

The language changes with culture and belief, but the core experience repeats: *"I was known completely and loved completely at the same time."*

There is no clipboard-wielding angel tapping a pen, waiting to scold you. There is no divine eye roll saying, "You again." There is welcome...there is recognition...there is a sense of home.

The psalmist hinted at this when he wrote: "Even though I walk through the valley of the shadow of death, I will fear no evil, for You are with me." (Psalm 23:4, NKJV/ESV)

Notice: death is described as a *shadow*, not the main reality. And the promise is not "You will avoid the valley," but "You will not walk it alone."

Jesus echoes the same assurance: "In My Father's house are many rooms...I go to prepare a place for you... that where I am, there you may be also." (John 14:2–3)

The heart of the message is not real estate. It is relationship: "Where I am... you will be with Me."

"More Real Than Real": The Quality of the Afterlife

One of the most striking features of near-death experiences is how often people say that the world they entered felt more real than this one.

Colors seem more alive... Sound has depth... Love is tangible... Knowing is immediate.

Some describe it like this: "This life felt like a shadow compared to *that*." "It was like going from black-and-white to color." "I didn't feel less conscious, I felt *fully* awake for the first time."

From a spiritual perspective, this makes sense. Scripture describes our current state as "seeing through a glass dimly," and the next as "face to face."

This life is important. It matters deeply. But it is not the final measure of reality. It is the training ground, the classroom, the pre-dawn of a far larger day.

It may sound odd, but many who return speak of being *reluctant* to come back; not because they hated life, but because what they tasted there felt like the fulfillment of every longing here.

That doesn't mean we should rush toward it or trivialize the gift of time we've been given. It simply means this: Whatever awaits is not less than the best experiences of love, joy, and peace you've known on earth...it is *more*.

"What if my deepest moments of joy and Presence here are previews, not anomalies?"

My Dad's Last Moments
This isn't just theory for me. One of the clearest glimpses I've ever had of what happens at the threshold of death came in the final moments of my dad's life.

My brother, Greg, and I were standing on each side of his bed at the hospice house. It was painful to see our father suffering, but even in that heaviness, there was a sense that these were holy minutes...time quietly gifted to us just before cancer ended his earthly journey.

As I write this, it is nearly twenty years to the day from that night, but the memory feels as close as yesterday.

Dad raised his right hand and began speaking about a ring... a circle. He was pointing to something, trying to describe what his eyes were seeing, but he couldn't quite find the words. It was as if he were looking into a reality we could not see and didn't yet have language for.

Greg leaned in and softly said, "Let go, dad. It will be alright."

Moments later, our father did something that stunned us both. He sat up in bed, reached his arms outward as if toward Someone, and repeated three words I will never forget: "Thank You, Jesus. Thank You, Jesus." In that moment, he finally felt safe enough to let go of his final breath.

Those three words carry power for many reasons, but the most significant for me is this: I had never heard my dad say the name *Jesus* before that moment.

My brother and I both knew, without a doubt, that even though we could not see Jesus in the room that night, our father could. His eyes were on the Prince of Peace.

It was as if, in those final breaths, the lights came on for him:
- pain giving way to Presence,
- fear giving way to trust,
- a lifetime of questions gathered into a single, grateful "Thank You."

I don't pretend to know the full story of what he was seeing. I only know this:

> He was not alone. And whatever, or rather *Whoever*, met him in that moment was so real, so kind, and so overwhelming in love that the only words he could find were gratitude.

When I think about what happens when we die, I can't separate it from that night. If a man who never spoke the name of Jesus in my hearing could meet Him with such clarity and peace in his final moments, then the Love waiting for us must be far more faithful and far more present than we have ever imagined.

A Brief Word on Science & NDEs

Science, by its nature, studies what can be measured in physical systems. The inner world of consciousness, especially at the edge of death, is not easy to put in a test tube. And yet, over the past few decades, researchers have done serious work examining near-death experiences in people whose brains, by all medical accounts, were in no state to be inventing vivid stories:

- individuals in cardiac arrest with no measurable heartbeat for several minutes,
- people under deep anesthesia with flat EEG readings,
- children too young to have absorbed complex doctrines,
- individuals who were blind from birth, describing their first reality of *seeing*, and matching what other NDEr's experienced.

Over and over, themes recur:
- a sense of leaving the body,
- being drawn into Light,
- encountering a loving Presence,
- being shown scenes of one's life,
- returning with transformed values—more love, less fear, less attachment to ego.

Researchers disagree on how to interpret these accounts. Some see them as purely brain-based phenomena. Others argue they point to consciousness existing beyond the brain. Either way, something important comes through: At the very moment we assume a person is "gone," many report being more lucid, more awake, and more *themselves* than they ever were here.

Science can't fully map heaven. But it can at least poke a few holes in the idea that death is mere oblivion. And when the data begins to sound strangely like the God of love Jesus described, we would be wise to pay attention.

"If even medicine is hearing echoes of Light in the stories of the nearly dead, what might that say about the One waiting for me?"

What About Judgment? (A Gentle Preview)

At this point, a question usually rises: "Okay... but what about judgment?" We've been taught to imagine some version of this scene:
- You stand in a massive celestial courtroom.
- Your life plays on a screen while everyone looks on.
- A stern Judge weighs the evidence, decides which pile you belong in, and slams the gavel.

No wonder so many are afraid. But remember:

- The God revealed in Jesus is not a two-faced deity; kind on earth, cruel in the afterlife.
- The Light that meets you is the same Light that has been chasing you all your life.

Jesus Himself said: "The Father judges no one, but has entrusted all judgment to the Son." And the Son says: "I did not come to condemn the world, but to save it."

Judgment, in the truest sense, is not God looking for a reason to reject you. It is God revealing reality: what was true, what was harmful, what was love, what was illusion.

This is where the life review comes in, which we'll explore in depth in the next chapter. For now, it's enough to say...after you die, you are not dragged into a courtroom. You are brought into clarity. And that clarity is held inside perfect love.

Death as a Wardrobe Change

One of my favorite ways I've heard it put is this: "Death is less an ending and more a wardrobe change." You are not losing your life; you are changing how you wear it.

Paul uses a similar image when he talks about being "clothed" with a heavenly dwelling. Picture it: You take off the heavy coat you've been wearing all winter, the one that was useful, necessary, even beautiful in its way, and you step into something lighter, made for where you're going next.

The unified life you've been living here; learning to walk in love, in trust, in awareness, does not get thrown away at death. It continues, expands, and deepens in a realm where the resistance is gone and the Light is unobstructed.

"If death is a wardrobe change, what kind of life am I 'weaving' into that next garment now?"

Living Now in Light of Then

All of this raises an important point: this chapter is not meant just to satisfy curiosity about the afterlife. It is meant to transform how you live *this* life. Because no matter how you interpret the seemingly conflicting themes in Scripture regarding what comes next, one thing still stands true: there is a real urgency in Scripture about responding to the Grace offered through the cross, and there are real consequences for hardening ourselves against it.

If:

- you are more than your body,
- you are held more securely than you realized,
- and the One waiting for you is pure love and truth.

Then:

- fear does not have to drive your choices,
- control does not have to be your god,
- and survival does not have to be your main goal.

You are free to:

- love more boldly,
- forgive more quickly,
- tell the truth more gently and courageously,
- follow the inner guidance of the Spirit even when it costs you comfort.

Because when you step through that final doorway, you will not be asked: "Did you play it safe?" You will be invited to see: "Did you learn to live from love? Did you let My Light shape you from the inside out? Did you become more real?" And wherever the answer is "not yet," you will be met with the same Love that has always been reshaping you.

Death does not end that process. It reveals it and carries it forward. Death, for many, is not described as an end, but as an unveiling. And one of the most consistent themes is the life review: seeing your life in light.

* * *

Key Insight

Death is not the opposite of life. It is a transition *within* life. You do not fall out of God when you die. You fall *into* God more fully.

- Your body returns to the earth.
- Your awareness passes through a threshold.
- You are met not by absence, but by Presence, by a Love that knows you completely and holds you completely.
- You awaken into a reality "more real than real," where the union you glimpsed here becomes clearer than ever.

Judgment, in that Light, is not divine rage but divine revelation. It is the beginning of deeper healing, not the end of your story.

Death is less a termination and more a transformation; less a wall and more a doorway into the same Light that has always been your true home.

Reflection Practice
Walking With Death in the Light of Love

Name Your Fears About Death: Take a blank page and write honestly: "When I think about death, I fear…" Don't censor yourself. Let every old teaching, image, or anxiety appear. Then, beside each line, add in smaller words: *"What if Love is kinder than this?"*

Remember Someone You've Lost: Bring to mind a person you love who has died. Imagine them not as "gone," but as more alive in the Presence of God. You might whisper: *"You are held in the same Love that is holding me. We are both in God, just in different rooms of the same house."*

A Breath Practice for Letting Go: When you feel anxious about endings, any endings, practice this: Inhale: "Held." Exhale: "Released." Let your body rehearse, in a tiny way, the ultimate trust: "I am held as I let go."

Prayer for the Last Breath (Now, While You're Breathing Fine): You might pray this quietly sometime when you're calm, simply as an act of trust:

"Holy One, when my final breath on this earth comes, let me remember what is true: that I am in You, that You are Light and Love, and that nothing, not even death ,can separate me from Your Presence. Teach me to live today the way I will see reality then, knowing I am held, knowing I am Yours."

Let death be a teacher, not a terror. Let it remind you that you are already living an eternal life, one that will pass through many doorways, but never fall out of the Hands that carry you.

CHAPTER EIGHTEEN

***

THE LIFE REVIEW

Seeing Your Story Through Love's Eyes

If death is a doorway into Presence, the life review is what happens when the lights come on. In Chapter 17, we explored what it means to cross the threshold of death; leaving the body, being met by Love, awakening into a reality "more real than real." But sooner or later, a quiet, serious question rises: *"What about my life? What about all the things I did and didn't do?"*

For many people, this is where fear quietly creeps back in. We imagine some final moment where everything about us is exposed and evaluated, and we're not sure how Love will look at us when nothing is hidden. A part of us still wonders: *Will God be disappointed? Will I have pushed His patience too far?*

But the heart of Scripture and near-death testimonies point to something very different and far more beautiful:

- The life review is not a trial, > it is a revelation.
- It is not God shaming you, > it is God showing you.
- Not to crush you with what you've done, > but to awaken you to what your life really meant.

"What if judgment is less God searching for a reason to reject me, and more God giving me the grace to finally see clearly?"

Some of what follows may stretch the edges of what you've been taught about death, judgment, and what comes next. I'm not asking you to agree with every detail or build a new theology overnight. I'm simply inviting you to stay curious; to hold a little space for the possibility that God's way of seeing us is far more loving, and far more healing, than many of us were ever told.

What if the moment we've most feared is not a scene of condemnation, but a moment of radical clarity in the Presence of Love?

Not Condemnation, but Clarity

Imagine standing in a Light that is utterly loving... utterly truthful... utterly incapable of lying to you. You are held in a Presence where you feel more safe and more exposed than you've ever felt in your existence. That is the atmosphere many near-death experiencers report during their life review.

Jesus hinted at this dynamic when He said, "There is nothing hidden that will not be disclosed, and nothing concealed that will not be brought out into the open." and again: "Everyone who does evil hates the light, and will not come into the light for fear that their deeds will be exposed. But whoever lives by the truth comes into the light, so that it may be seen plainly what they have done."

Notice the point is not humiliation, the point is *seeing plainly*.

In the life review, this is what has been described: your entire life is brought into the Light, not as a list of charges. But as a living tapestry of choices, consequences, and unseen ripples. You see:
- the obvious moments and the small ones,
- the prayers you remember and the ones you forgot you prayed,
- the wounds you carried and the wounds you caused.

And through it all, you feel one unshakable reality: "I am completely known...and I am still completely loved." The truth may pierce. But it does not abandon.

Experiencing What You Gave

One of the most consistent features reported in near-death experiences is this: In the life review, you do not just *watch* what you did. You *feel* it...from the other side.

If you spoke a harsh word, you experience that moment again, not only from your own viewpoint, but from the heart of the person who received it. If you showed kindness to a stranger, you feel the lift it gave them on a day you never knew was heavy. If you encouraged someone who was quietly drowning in despair, you feel the way your words became air in their lungs.

It's as if God gently says: "Let Me show you your life, not just from *inside* your own skin, but from *inside* the lives you touched."

This is what Jesus meant when He said, 'Whatever you did to the least of these, you did to Me." (Matthew 25:40-paraphrased)

Every action touches more than one heart. In the life review, you experience those touches as if they happened to you. This is not divine revenge. It is divine empathy.

You are being invited into God's own way of seeing: how deeply connected we all are, how no moment is small, how love and harm both ripple farther than we realized.

"If I am going to feel my choices through others' hearts one day, how might that change how I speak and act today?"

The Ripple Effect: Seeds, Fruit, and Echoes
Scripture has been telling this story all along:
- Whatever a person sows, that will he also reap.
- With the measure you use, it will be measured back to you.
- By their fruits you will know them.

We have often heard these verses as threats. *But think of them as descriptions of how reality works.*

In the life review, you see:
- that every word was a seed,
- every action a cause,
- every attitude an echo.

You watch:
- how a careless comment planted shame that affected someone's choices for years,
- how a simple act of generosity set off a chain of kindness you never saw,
- how your presence—peaceful or chaotic—shaped the atmosphere of a room.

One person described it like this: "I saw how my life had grown like a tree; every choice was a branch, every branch bore fruit, and that fruit fell into other lives."

In that Light, you cannot say, "It didn't matter." You see that it did. And yet, the One showing all of this to you is not gloating. He is not saying, "See what you did, you failure." He is saying: *"This is how powerful you were. This is how much your life mattered. This is how seriously I took your freedom."*

It is justice as *understanding*, not as mockery.

The Role of Forgiveness in the Life Review

Here is where one of the most beautiful mysteries appears: Forgiveness changes how your past is felt in the Light. Jesus said, "Forgive, and you will be forgiven...for with the measure you use, it will be measured back to you."

We often shrink that into a bargain: "I'll forgive so I don't get in trouble." But in the life review, you see the deeper meaning:

- When you forgive someone, you are not pretending the wound didn't happen. You are releasing the *energetic weight* of it into God.
- When someone forgives you, they are not erasing the event. They are transforming the "vibration" of it with love.

So what does this mean as you see your life in the Light? The event remains in your timeline, but it no longer radiates the same pain and poison. Love changes the *quality* of the memory, the way it lives in your nervous system, your heart, and even your relationships.

You're not erasing history; you're *transmuting* it. You still see the truth of what happened. You still feel, from the other person's side, what your choices caused. But if they have sincerely released you into love; if they have forgiven, there is a softness in how that moment is experienced.

The wound is no longer an open, infected cut. It is a scar; real, remembered, but healed. Forgiveness doesn't erase the truth. It changes the atmosphere in which truth is received.

The same is true in reverse: where *you* have forgiven others, the heavy energy of resentment no longer distorts your own life review. You see what happened, but you see it through the lens of mercy you've chosen.

You begin to understand why Jesus taught forgiveness so insistently, not as a rule to appease a touchy God. But as a way of healing the field in which all of us will one day stand together in the Light.

"If my future clarity will include the grace I've chosen to give and receive, what kind of atmosphere am I creating around my memories now?"

"Godly Sorrow": When Regret Becomes Healing

Let's be honest, some moments in the life review will hurt. Not because God is hurting you, but because seeing the truth, without self-justification, can sting.

You may feel what Scripture calls "godly sorrow", not the shame that says, "I am trash," but the deep ache that says, "Oh... that was not love. I wish I had chosen differently."

In that space:
- you may feel grief over missed opportunities to love,
- pain over ways you wounded others out of your own wounds,
- regret for years spent chasing illusions.

But here is the crucial difference: You are not left alone inside that sorrow. The very Light that shows you your life is the Love that holds you while you see it.

The Presence says, in effect: "Yes, this was real. Yes, it mattered. And I have never stopped working to redeem it." Where on earth shame might say, "Look what you did, you're hopeless," in the life review, Love says, "Look what happened, and see how I can heal."

Your sorrow becomes consent. You agree with Love. You let go of excuses and self-deception. You say, "Yes, this was not who I truly am in You." That "yes" is not condemnation. It is the beginning of transformation.

The Life Review Is for You, Not for God

One more freeing truth: God is not learning anything new in your life review. You are. God does not need to replay your life to "check the record." *He has walked every moment with you.* The review is not to inform God. It is to awaken *you*. You finally see:

- where you agreed with Love and where you resisted,
- where you believed lies about yourself and others,
- where you lived from your true self and where you lived from fear, ego, or illusion.

In that seeing, something crucial happens: You and God now agree about what is true. And where you agree with Love, healing can go all the way down. Think of it like a spiritual MRI: God is not shaming you for having a fracture. He is showing you where the fracture is so it can be set, healed, and strengthened.

The life review is less like a verdict and more like a diagnosis in the arms of the Great Physician.

Reflection Box: The Mirror of Truth

In this life, you glimpse the mirror of truth in quiet moments; a pang of conscience, a nudge to apologize, a sense that you're living smaller than what Love is inviting you into.

In the life review, you step fully in front of that mirror. You see your story with all the filters off; not through shame, not through self-justification, but through the steady gaze of Love.

The mirror does not lie, but it also does not hate what it reflects. It reveals to restore.

To live wisely is to visit that mirror now...to let small daily reviews with God prepare you for the great, all-encompassing one later.

The more you practice truth in love here, the less foreign that Light will feel there.

Practicing Your Life Review Now

One of the most beautiful things about this whole picture is that you don't have to wait for death to start living in light of it. You can begin a gentle, daily "mini life review" right now. Not as morbid obsession.

Not as self-beating. But as friendship with the truth.

You might ask at the end of a day: *"If I saw today from the other side, what moments would I be most grateful for? Where would I wish I had loved more freely?"*

This simple practice doesn't earn you points. It familiarizes you with the Light. When the day comes that you step through the final doorway, you will not be meeting a stranger. You'll be meeting a Presence you've been learning to trust for years.

* * *

Key Insight

The life review is not a cosmic shaming session. It is Love walking you back through your own story until you see it truthfully from every side.

You experience your choices from the inside *and* from the hearts of those you affected.

You see the ripples of your life; both the harm and the healing.

You feel sorrow where you withheld love and joy where you freely gave it.

You discover that forgiveness, given and received, changes how the past is held in the Light.

God doesn't seem to be using the review to decide whether to love you, but using it to complete love's work in you. Judgment, in this sense, is not retribution. It is revelation that restores.

The life review is not humiliation...it's clarity. And clarity naturally raises a deeper question: what is divine justice really for?

Reflection Practice
Living Today in the Light of Tomorrow

1. **A Gentle Evening Review**: Before sleep, take a few slow breaths and ask:

    o "Where today did I live in alignment with Love?"
    o "Where did I pull back, self-protect, or wound?"

Don't spiral into shame. Simply acknowledge what you see while resting in God's presence.

You might pray: "Thank You for every place love flowed today. Heal and transform every place it didn't."

2. **See Through Another's Eyes**: Think of one interaction that still bothers you; either because you were hurt or because you're not proud of how you acted. Ask the Spirit to show you that moment from the other person's perspective. Notice what you feel. Then ask: "What would love look like here, both for them and for me?"

3. **Release a Weight from the Past:** Bring to mind a memory that still feels heavy. It could be something you did or something done to you. Imagine placing that memory into the Light of God and pray: "I don't deny what happened. But I refuse to carry it apart from You any longer. Where I need to forgive, help me forgive. Where I need forgiveness, I receive it. Hold this memory in Your love and heal it."

4. **Ask a Life-Review Question in Real Time**: When you face a decision, large or small, pause and ask: *"If I saw this moment again in the Light, what choice would I be grateful I made?"* You won't always get it "perfect," but this simple question begins to align your present with your future clarity.

As you walk with the idea of the life review, remember:

You are not walking toward a God eager to condemn you. You are moving toward a God eager to show you, heal you, and bring you more fully into the truth of who you are in Him.

CHAPTER NINETEEN

***

DIVINE JUSTICE: REVELATION, NOT RETRIBUTION

Consequences as Clarity, Not Condemnation

There is a reason the desire for vengeance rises so naturally in the human heart when we are wronged. It is not because we are inherently violent or morally defective. It is because, at a soul level, we know that justice is woven into the structure of reality itself.

Not punishment -> balance. Not wrath -> restoration.

Even Jesus pointed to this inner knowing when He taught "...with the measure you use, it will be measured back to you."

This is not a threat; it is a description of spiritual cause and effect. The ego distorts this truth into the urge to strike back, to restore balance by force: *"They hurt me, so I must hurt them."*

But the deeper self understands a more profound principle: Every action carries an echo, and every echo eventually returns. This is the meaning behind God's words, "Vengeance is Mine."

Not: "I will finally unleash My rage."

But: "Leave justice to Me. I will reveal all things in the Light."

"What if divine justice is less about God finally getting mad enough to punish, and more about God being endlessly committed to making all things true?"

Justice Woven Into Reality
Whether we realize it or not, we experience this moral structure every day.

- A life of bitterness tends to grow isolating.
- A life of generosity tends to draw support.
- A life of deception tends to collapse under its own weight.
- A life of truth, though sometimes costly, becomes a place of safety.

Paul summarized this universal law when he wrote, "Whatever a person sows, that shall he also reap." (Galatians 6:7) This is not divine retaliation. It is divine precision. Every word is a seed. Every action a cause. Every moment a ripple.

Jesus described it plainly:

> "By their fruits you will know them." (Matthew 7:20)

Divine justice, then, is not God arbitrarily picking winners and losers. It is God allowing the full truth of what we have sown to be revealed, for our awakening and healing.

"In the Life Review, No One Is Punished. Everyone Is Shown."

In Chapter 18, we explored the life review in depth. Let's return to its core insight, because it is the clearest window into divine justice.

Across countless Near-Death Experiences and ancient spiritual traditions, one truth emerges again and again: In the life review, no one is punished. Everyone is shown. Jesus hinted at this when He said,

> "Everyone who does evil hates the light, and will not come into the light for fear that their deeds will be exposed. But whoever lives by the truth comes into the light, so that it may be seen plainly what they have done." (John 3:20–21 NIV)

In the life review, the soul is brought into that Light. Not to be condemned, but to see. A person experiences their actions from the perspective of every life they touched; not symbolically, but exactly as those people felt it, both the pain and the joy. This isn't retribution. This is perfect clarity.

Clarity heals. Clarity transforms. Clarity awakens.

Paul pointed toward this same mystery when he wrote, "Each person's work will be shown for what it is, because the Day will bring it to light... the fire will reveal the quality of each person's work." (1 Corinthians 3:13 NIV)

The "fire" is not punishment. It is illumination. Divine justice does not need to humiliate or destroy you. It only needs to show you what has always been true.

The Ripple Effect of Choice

The Light does not only reveal the moments we remember. It reveals the *chain reaction* of our choices:

- The harsh word that altered someone's inner world.
- Their hurt spilling into another moment.
- The kindness that uplifted someone who passed that kindness onward.
- The silent, hidden choices that shaped unseen futures.

What looked to you like a small, forgettable moment is shown as: a seed...that became a branch...that bore fruit... that fell into other lives.

The fruit of our choices always returns to us; not as random fate, but as understanding.

"If I am going to see and feel my choices from every angle one day, how might that change how I plant seeds now?"

Where Forgiveness Enters the Equation

Forgiveness is one of the most misunderstood powers on Earth. When someone truly forgives you, they do not erase the past, they change the *energetic weight* of it.

Jesus said, "Forgive, and you will be forgiven... for with the measure you use, it will be measured to you." (Luke 6:37–38)

This means:
- Forgiveness heals the wound.
- Forgiveness transforms the vibration.
- Forgiveness softens the ripple.
- Forgiveness changes the way consequences are experienced in the Light.

In your life review, although you will still see the truth of what you caused, you will not feel the full, raw weight of another person's pain if they have already released it into love. Forgiveness doesn't erase the truth; it heals the field through which truth is received.

Forgiveness is one of the greatest gifts you can give someone, and the peace that flows from genuine forgiveness saturates both hearts.

In the same way, where *you* have forgiven others, the heavy gravity of resentment no longer distorts your own experience. You see clearly what happened, but without the poison of ongoing hatred.

Divine justice honors forgiveness. Grace you have given and grace you have received both shape how your story is held in the Light.

A Narrative Glimpse: The Life Review

He found himself standing in a light that seemed alive, a light that held him with the gentleness of God's own Presence. There was no fear, no accusation, only the overwhelming sense of being fully known.

Then the Light showed him his life. Not in flashes, but in *feeling*.

He felt his childhood laughter through the hearts of those who loved him. He felt his acts of kindness lifting spirits on days he never knew were heavy. He felt the sting of every harsh word he had spoken; not as punishment, but as the wound carried by the one who heard it.

He saw how a single choice opened into another, and another, and another...

- A sigh of impatience darkening someone's morning.
- A smile brightening someone's entire week.
- A ripple becoming a wave becoming a life. He remembered Jesus' words:

"Whatever is hidden is meant to be disclosed, and whatever is concealed is meant to be brought into the open." (Mark 4:22 - paraphrased)

He was not condemned. He was awakened.

Free Will in Life -> and Beyond

God never removes our choices...not in this life...not in the next. Choice is the engine of soul-growth. Every decision shapes us: some expanding us...some humbling us...some breaking us open, but all instructing us.

Jesus declared a profound spiritual law:

> "Whatever you bind on earth will be bound in heaven, and whatever you loose on earth will be loosed in heaven." (Matthew 18:18)

What we cling to, we carry. What we release, releases us.

Death does not override our freedom; it reveals the consequences of our freedom with love and truth. We have just as much free will after death as we do on earth.

In the life review:
- you are not forced into remorse,
- you are not coerced to change,
- you are simply shown the truth...and then you choose.

The same freedom exists:
- to awaken or to remain asleep,
- to learn or to resist,
- to accept or to deny the consequences.

But when the soul sees truth clearly, clarity naturally leads it toward harmony. Just as a musician corrects a sour note once they hear it clearly, the soul seeks to heal whatever has fallen out of tune. This is true justice: freedom paired with understanding, never compulsion.

Self-Chosen Separation: The True Nature of Hell

I believe one of the most misunderstood ideas in all of spirituality is the nature of "hell." Not the cultural version. Not the theatrical, fear-based version. The actual spiritual reality of what separation from God *feels* like.

Scripture teaches plainly that nothing can separate us from the love of God (Romans 8:38–39). Yet this does not mean a soul cannot close itself off to the *experience* of that love.

Hell is not something God inflicts. Hell is something a soul chooses when it refuses the truth shown to it.

In the life review, every soul stands in the Presence of perfect love and perfect clarity. Nothing is hidden, nothing is condemned, and nothing is forced. But the soul must still make a choice: *Do I accept the truth of what I created? Or do I deny it to preserve the ego?*

When a soul denies truth, clings to illusion, or rejects understanding, a spiritual dissonance arises. It is not God withdrawing from the soul...it is the soul withdrawing from God.

Jesus described this when He said, "People loved darkness rather than light because their deeds were evil." (John 3:19)

The Light reveals. Love heals. Truth liberates.

But when a soul resists truth, that resistance becomes its suffering. Hell is not *primarily* a place. It is a condition; the pain of resisting Reality. The more a soul clings to illusion, the more torment it feels, because illusion cannot survive the Presence of perfect truth.

As C.S. Lewis wrote,
"The doors of hell are locked from the inside."

Not by God. By the soul protecting its false self. And yet, even here, mercy remains. No soul can eternally resist the Light. Love is stronger. Truth is gentler but more relentless. God is endlessly patient. And the soul is designed for reunion.

While a soul may choose separation, is that separation its destiny?

Will not eventually, through revelation, not force...every soul will return to the Light it came from?

Is hell the final destination of the wicked or is it the healing space for the resistant?

In the endlessness of divine mercy, will not every soul one day awaken willingly into the Presence of God?

The Lake of Fire: A Biblical Image of Purification, Not Condemnation?

The phrase "lake of fire" can stir fear in anyone who was raised to believe God created a place of endless torment. But the biblical language, especially when read through the lens of Christ's teaching and much of early Christian understanding, reveals something far different.

Fire in Scripture symbolizes purification, not torture. "Our God is a consuming fire." (Hebrews 12:29)

"He will baptize you with the Holy Spirit and with fire." (Matthew 3:11 NLT)

"The fire will test each one's work." (1 Cor. 3:13 -paraphrased) Fire reveals what is true and dissolves what is false.

Revelation calls it "the second death." The second death is the death of:

- ego
- deception
- hatred
- rebellion
- and every illusion that cannot endure God's Presence.

It is not the torture of souls, but the end of deception.

Jesus said it was "...prepared for the devil and his angels." (Matthew 25:41)

This does not mean prepared primarily to punish humans, but to dismantle the entire system of deception, everything characterized as "the adversary."

If justice is revelation, then it is meant to heal, not harden. From here, we step into the promise that growth doesn't stop—life in God continues to unfold.

Early Christianity often saw the fire as restorative. For teachers like Gregory of Nyssa and Isaac the Syrian, fire was God's healing Presence, burning away all that is unlike love.

The lake of fire aligns with the life review.

- Both reveal truth.
- Both purify illusion.
- Both restore what is real.

In this sense, the lake of fire is the final purification of all that is false, the triumph of truth, not the eternal torment of souls.

Reflection: The Light That Shows All Things

At some level, everyone fears being "found out." We worry that if the full truth about us were ever revealed, it would be the end of us. But in the end, the Light that shows all things is the same Love that has held all things from the beginning.

Nothing in you will be revealed that God has not already seen. Nothing will surprise Him. The only one who will be surprised is *you*, by how deeply your life mattered, by how far your choices reached, and by how unwavering His mercy has been.

To live wisely now is to begin walking toward that Light on purpose:
- telling the truth a little sooner,
- forgiving a little quicker,
- releasing what you've been binding yourself to,
- and daring to believe that justice and mercy are not opposites in God, but two hands of the same Love.

If justice is revelation, then it is meant to heal, not harden. And wouldn't this mean that the story doesn't end at judgment, and that growth will continue in God?

What if eternity is not static perfection, but endless awakening into Love?

* * *

Key Insight

Divine justice is not retribution but revelation; not punishment but perspective; not condemnation but understanding.

Every action carries an echo.
Every echo eventually returns.
Every soul is shown the truth of its own choices in the Light of Love.

The "fire" of God does not exist to destroy the true self, but to dissolve everything that is not rooted in love.

In the end, does not every soul return home transformed by the truth it has seen, exactly as Jesus taught?

Reflection Practice
<u>Walking With Justice Without Fear</u>
Notice Where You Want Payback
Bring to mind a situation where you secretly (or not so secretly) want someone to "get what's coming." Without shaming yourself, sit with that feeling and pray: "Holy Love, I don't minimize what happened. But I ask for justice that heals, not harm that multiplies harm. Show me how You see this."

Name What You're Binding (and Loosing)
Complete these sentences in a journal:
- "I've been binding myself to this story about me: _____."
- "I've been binding myself to this story about them: _____."

Then pray: "Whatever is not true, I loose into Your hands. Teach me to live aligned with what *is* true."

Invite Refining Without Terror
In a quiet moment, whisper: "Refiner of my soul, I invite Your fire, not to punish me, but to burn away what is false. Let only love remain."

Notice any resistance that rises. Offer even that resistance into the Presence.

Practice a Small Daily Review
At the end of the day, ask:
- "Where today did I sow love?"
- "Where did I sow fear or illusion?"

Thank God for every seed of love. For the other places, simply say:

"I see it now. Heal this, and teach me a better way."

You are not walking toward a courtroom where Love might reject you. You are walking toward a Light where Love will finally show you the whole truth...so that nothing false remains between you and the One who has been your home all along.

CHAPTER TWENTY

***

ETERNAL GROWTH IN GOD

Becoming More Forever

There is a quiet question that lingers behind all our talk of heaven, judgment, and the life to come: *"Then what?"*

If we awaken into the Presence of God...if we are healed, restored, and brought home...if every tear is wiped away and all is made new...*Then what?*

Many people were handed an image of eternity that secretly sounds more like an endless church service or a cosmic retirement plan:

- a cloud,
- a harp,
- an eternal hymn sing,
- everyone politely happy and strangely flat.

If we're honest, part of us wonders: *"Won't that... eventually get boring?"*

The good news is this: boredom is not in the nature of the living God. When a person realizes the Light within them, who they truly are, boredom simply can't survive.

The same God who created galaxies, DNA, music, humor, colors we haven't even seen yet, and the wild complexity of your own heart is not about to run out of ideas at the one place we're supposed to be most alive.

"What if eternity is not an endless freeze-frame, but an endless unfolding?"

Scripture whispers this in a thousand ways:

- "Of His kingdom there will be no end."
- "Now we know in part…"
- We go "from glory to glory…"
- In the coming ages, God will "show the incomparable riches of His grace…"

This is the language of movement, not stagnation; of growth, not spiritual retirement. Heaven is not the end of the journey. It is the end of the physical limitations that cloud our sight, and the beginning of eternal growth in God.

The Ache for "More" as a Clue

All through this book, we've returned to that inner ache; the sense that there is "more" to God, more to life, more to you. That ache is not a flaw. It is a signature, an imprint of our Creator. Even after profound moments of awakening, something in you still senses:

- there is more to discover,
- more to become,
- more love to receive and to give.

On earth, we often misread that ache and try to satisfy it with:

- more success,
- more experiences,
- more stimulation,
- more spiritual information.

But underneath it all is a simpler longing: *I want to know the One from whom all this came. And I want to keep discovering, forever."*

That ache is not cancelled in eternity. It is finally met. The difference is: here, the ache is often mixed with frustration and limitation; there, the same ache becomes delight…an endless invitation into depths of God that no finite age can exhaust.

"Of His Kingdom There Will Be No End"

When the angel announced Jesus' birth, the promise was simple and staggering:

> *"Of His kingdom there will be no end."*

We often reduce that to mean, "His rule keeps going forever." But His "kingdom" is not just rule; it is *reality as God intends it*...life in union, love, and truth.

For there to be no end to that kingdom means:

- no end to the unfolding of love,
- no end to the discovery of God's heart,
- no end to the creativity, beauty, and joy that flow from union.

If eternity were static, everyone frozen at one level of awareness or joy, then in a sense, the kingdom *would* have an end. It would reach a point and stop.

But if the kingdom is a living, expanding reality...God sharing God's own life with creation, then of His kingdom there truly is *no end* because: there is no end to God and no ceiling on how much we can awaken into God.

You don't become "equally omniscient" with God. But you do keep growing *in* God, without fear of loss, without running out of time.

"Now We Know in Part..." -> Forever
Paul wrote: "Now we know in part..."

For many, that verse has been used to say, "Relax, you just can't know much now." But tucked inside is a breathtaking implication: If even the greatest saints, mystics, and thinkers only "know in part" *here*, and if God is infinite, then even in the ages to come, we will always be moving from *part* to *more*.

You don't go from partial knowledge to total comprehension of the Infinite in a single leap. You go from:

- glory to glory,
- light to greater light,
- depth to greater depth.

Imagine spending a thousand years exploring one facet of God's wisdom and realizing you've barely begun. Imagine understanding love so deeply that you can hardly bear its beauty...then being invited deeper still.

Not as pressure. As joy.

"If I will be learning and expanding in Love forever, can I relax a little about 'having it all figured out' now?"

No Spiritual Flatlining

One of the subtle fears about eternity is that you'll somehow lose your *you-ness*; your distinct personality, your story, your quirks. But union with God is not absorption into a bland spiritual soup. It is *communion*.

- you fully you,
- me fully me,
- all of us fully alive in God,
- with nothing false left.

Sin, shame, fear, illusion, egoic masks, those fall away. But the real you, the you God dreamed from before the foundation of the world, is more alive, not less.

In eternity:

- Your individuality isn't erased; it's clarified.
- Your gifts are not shelved; they're finally free of distortion.
- Your capacity to love is not exhausted; it's continually expanded.

Heaven is not soul-flattening. It is soul-deepening. Think of the most alive version of yourself you've tasted for a moment on earth; those rare times you felt fully present, fully loving, fully at peace.

Eternal growth in God means: that version of you is not a rare exception. It becomes the baseline, from which you keep growing.

Creation as Classroom, Eternity as Home (and School)

Life on earth is not a meaningless test. It is a classroom, and a womb. Here you learn:

- trust in the middle of unknowing,
- love in the presence of difference and difficulty,
- surrender in the presence of limitation,
- faith in the presence of unanswered questions.

These are not wasted skills. They are the foundations of how you will relate to God and others forever. In eternity: You are at home; no more separation, no more fundamental fear. And yet, you are still a learner, explorer, co-creator.

Those who briefly cross over in NDEs often speak of:
- realms of beauty and knowledge,
- learning places,
- landscapes that are more real and more symbolic than anything here,
- music and color that communicate wisdom and love beyond words.

While we hold these testimonies lightly and test them, they consistently harmonize with the scriptural vision:

> "Eye has not seen, ear has not heard, nor has it entered into the heart of man, what God has prepared for those who love Him." (1 Corinthians 2:9)

Prepared–not as a static reward to stare at, but as an ever-unfolding life to participate in.

From Glory to Glory (Without Rushing)

Paul uses another phrase that belongs here: "We are being transformed from glory to glory..."

On earth, that often feels like: two steps forward, one step back, long plateaus, sudden breakthroughs, seasons of fire and seasons of rest. In eternity, the *struggle* component falls away. No more wrestling with sin, trauma, or terror of abandonment. But the *movement* remains.

God is not in a hurry. Eternity is not a productivity contest. There is no spiritual FOMO. No fear that someone else is "getting ahead of you forever."

Instead: you grow at the pace of love...you awaken at the pace your soul can bear...you explore at the pace of joy, not anxiety.

The only "urgency" in eternity is the joyful urgency of love; the way you can't wait to discover more of someone you adore.

Eternal Relationships, Eternal Stories

If justice is restorative (Chapter 19), then relationships are not thrown away like broken tools. They are healed, clarified, and re-founded in truth.

Imagine:

- meeting again those you hurt and those who hurt you, not in shame, but in a light where everything has been named, forgiven, and purified.
- seeing how God has woven all your stories together, not to excuse harm, but to bring forth redemption you couldn't imagine.
- co-laboring with beings you once only read about, saints, ancestors, friends you haven't met yet, in a universe where all work is joy and all purpose is love.

Your story doesn't evaporate after death. It continues, now woven into the larger story of God's ongoing creativity.

If there are new worlds to be shaped, new dimensions of beauty to be expressed, new ways for the Divine Life to be mirrored...you'll have a part to play.

How Eternal Growth Changes Life Now

You might ask: "This is beautiful, but what does it change while I'm still here?" More than we realize.

If you think eternity is essentially static, everyone either *done* or *done for*, then this life becomes:

- a frantic scramble to "get it right" before the clock runs out,
- a sorting exercise more than a growth journey,
- a place where fear is the main motivator.

But if you see eternity as continued awakening in God:

- you can relax your perfectionism, growth doesn't end at the grave;
- you can take this life seriously but not hysterically;
- you can focus less on "earning a spot" and more on learning to love.

This doesn't make this life unimportant. It makes it *foundational.* Every act of love is already participation in eternal life. Every moment of presence is already a rehearsal for eternity. Every time you choose truth over illusion, you are tuning your being to the reality you will live in forever.

Eternal growth in God means: You are not preparing for a foreign country. You are learning the language of your true homeland, one choice at a time.

"If I really believed that this journey continues forever in Love, how might that soften my fear of death, and how might it deepen my commitment to love today?"

If God is infinite, then life in God is infinite—always deeper, always more alive. Now we bring that eternity-home into today: everyday awakening.

* * *

Key Insight

Eternity is not an endless pause. It is an endless unfolding.

"Of His kingdom there will be no end" means there is no end to the ways God can share His life with you.

"Now we know in part" means there is always more to learn, but never a moment when you are unloved as you are.

"From glory to glory" does not stop at the grave; it continues in realms beyond our imagining.

Heaven is not spiritual retirement. It is the end of separation and the beginning of eternal growth in God; you becoming more fully yourself, forever, in the Infinite Love that has always been your home.

Reflection Practice

Living Now in Light of Forever

1. **Gently Release the "Static Heaven" Image**: Take a moment and write down the picture of heaven you grew up with; clouds, harps, endless sermons, boredom, fear, whatever it was. Then underneath, write: "Of His kingdom

there will be no end. Love is endlessly creative. My true home will not be less alive than this world, but more."

Sit with that. Let it begin to loosen old images.

2. **Ask the Eternal Question in a Present Moment**: Sometime today, pause in a very ordinary moment; washing dishes, driving, talking with someone, and ask: *"If this moment is part of my eternal story, how might I be a little more present, a little more loving, right here?"*

3. **Bless Your Future Self in God**: Place a hand on your heart and pray: "Eternal Love, thank You that my story doesn't end in fear or emptiness, but in You. I bless the 'me' I will become in Your Presence. Teach me now to live in the same direction; toward love...toward truth... toward You."

4. **Let Go of the Need to "Arrive"**: When you catch yourself thinking, "I should be further along by now," gently remind yourself: "I am in process, and process is holy. Growth does not stop at death. I am safe to keep learning." Let that soften your inner pressure and open you again to grace.

PART VI: LIVING THE REALIZATION

Bringing Heaven to Earth

By now, you've seen the arc: Awakening to the Light within; Healing the split inside; Learning to walk in alignment and guidance; Seeing death not as an ending but as a doorway; Discovering that justice, love, and growth continue forever in God.

But if all of this stayed as *beautiful ideas* about God, the soul, and eternity, it would miss the point. The real question is: *"What does any of this look like on a Tuesday afternoon with laundry in the dryer and three notifications buzzing on my phone?"*

Part VI is about that. This is where heaven stops being a distant location and becomes a present orientation. Where "light" stops being a metaphor and becomes a way of moving through your day. Where prayer stops being something you only "go do" and becomes the air you breathe.

In this final section, we'll explore:
- how to let awakening become a lifestyle, not just an experience,
- how to bring presence into ordinary moments,
- how to live as a person of Light in a world still confused about itself,
- how to walk in peace without checking out of life,
- how to experience more of those moments when you feel deeply, undeniably alive; without an added substance☺,
- how to keep saying "yes" to growth, gently and steadily, until your last breath (and beyond).

You are not called to escape the world, but to walk in it differently, as someone who knows where home is, and carries that atmosphere with them.

This is what it means to *live the realization*.

CHAPTER TWENTY-ONE

* * *

EVERYDAY AWAKENING

Making the Ordinary Sacred (Without Making Life Weird)

Most people imagine "spiritual awakening" happening on mountain-tops, in monasteries, or in dramatic moments of crisis. And sometimes it does. But for most of us, the real work of awakening happens in:

- traffic,
- email,
- grocery lines,
- staff meetings,
- bedtime routines,
- awkward conversations,
- and the quiet in-between spaces of everyday life.

If awakening can't reach into those moments, it's not the kind of awakening Jesus modeled. He didn't float through life three feet off the ground. He walked dusty roads, ate with friends, faced interruptions, dealt with critics, and lived inside a very ordinary human body.

Yet He lived awake.

He lived from union; seeing the Father in all things, moving with the Spirit's flow, bringing heaven's atmosphere into every interaction.

Everyday awakening is simply this: Letting the Light you've remembered shape the way you move through your actual life. Not a different life. This one.

Spirituality Without the Spotlight
You don't have to: quit your job, move to a cabin in the woods, or carry around a permanent half-smile so people know you're "at peace

now." In fact, if your awakening requires a spotlight to prove it's happening, something has already drifted off-center.

Everyday awakening is quieter, humbler, and far more practical. It sounds like:

- "I'm going to pause before I respond."
- "I'm going to forgive quicker than I would have last year."
- "I'm going to invite God into this email, this meeting, this drive across town."
- "I'm going to treat the person in front of me as if they matter as much as they actually do."

It looks like:

- a softer tone,
- a slower judgment,
- a quicker gratitude,
- a more honest "I'm sorry,"
- a more frequent, "Help me see this with Your eyes."

You won't always get it "right." But the difference is: you notice. And when you notice, you return.

"What if my most spiritual moments are not the ones that feel dramatic, but the ones where love quietly wins inside me?"

"Pray Without Ceasing": As Awareness, Not Performance

Paul gave one of the most intimidating commands in Scripture: "Pray without ceasing."

If you grew up imagining prayer only as formal words, eyes closed, hands folded, this sounds impossible. But think of prayer less as a scheduled activity and more as a steady orientation of heart.

To "pray without ceasing" is to:

- keep turning your attention toward God, again and again,
- carry on a quiet conversation under the surface of your day,
- allow awareness of Presence to walk with you into everything.

It might look like:

- "Be with me in this," whispered under your breath before a meeting.
- "Thank You for this," breathed out while doing dishes.

- "Help me see them like You do," prayed while listening to a difficult person.
- "I don't know what to do, but I'm here," admitted in the middle of confusion.

Prayer becomes less like a phone call you sometimes make and more like an open line that's never hung up. You're not always talking, but you're always *connected*.

Tiny Altars in a Busy Day

One practical way to live everyday awakening is to build small "altars" into your routine; simple, repeatable cues that bring you back to the Now and to God. This might be:

First Light – Before you reach for your phone, place a hand over your heart and say, "Here I am. Thank You for this day. Lead me in Light."

Doorways – Every time you walk through a doorway, let it remind you: "I carry Light into this room."

Water Moments – While washing your hands or taking a shower, breathe, "Wash my mind. Clear my heart. Let only love remain."

Red Lights – Instead of resenting every stop, use them as 10-second sanctuaries: "I am held. Love is here."

None of these require more time. They ask for more *awareness*. Over time, these little practices stitch the day together into one continuous yes.

Bringing the Inner GPS Into Ordinary Decisions

In earlier chapters, we explored the idea of an inner GPS, the quiet guidance of Ruach, Spirit, Presence, within you. Everyday awakening means: You don't just consult that GPS for "big" decisions. You bring it into the small ones too. Not in a neurotic way, "Spirit, should I choose the blue socks or the black ones?" But in a relational way:

"Is this conversation mine to have right now?"

"Am I saying 'yes' out of love or out of fear of disappointing?"

"Is this extra commitment aligned with my actual calling, or is it ego trying to feel important?"

Sometimes the answer comes as a clear inner sense: a yes, a no, or a gentle "not now." Sometimes it comes as peace...or a lack of it. Sometimes it comes as a Scripture that rises in your mind, a memory, or a subtle tightening in your chest.

The point is not to decode every feeling. The point is to stay in dialogue. You're not asking for a detailed map. You're trusting a faithful Guide for the next step.

When You Forget (Because You Will)
There will be days when:
- you snap at someone you love,
- you spiral into anxiety,
- you numb out instead of tuning in,
- you binge your favorite distraction instead of bringing your heart to God.

On those days, the ego loves to say: "Well, that's it. So much for all that 'awakening' talk. You've obviously failed."

But everything you've learned so far has been preparing you for this truth: Awakening is not a straight line. It is a rhythm of remembering and returning.

You don't "fall out" of spirituality because you had a bad day. You simply drifted from awareness. And the moment you notice and say, "I'm off, but I want to come back," you're already returning. In fact, those "failure" moments often deepen your compassion, for yourself and others, more than any "perfect" day ever could.

"What if the most important moment is not when I get it wrong, but when I notice...and what I do next?"

A Little Humor Helps
Let's be honest: On paper, "walking in peace, presence, and love" sounds beautiful. In practice, it sometimes looks like:
- trying to remember a breath prayer while your kid is asking you 14 questions in 9 seconds,
- choosing not to send the perfectly crafted angry text you *really* want to send,

- whispering "Lord, have mercy" in the grocery store when you're on aisle 7 and just realized you forgot the one thing you came for.

Awakening is not an event you complete—it's a life you practice. Next, we'll gather it all into what it looks like to live realized—steady, radiant, and whole.

It's okay to laugh at yourself. Sometimes the holiest thing you can do is smile, shrug, and say: "Well... that was not my finest enlightened moment. Thank You that Your Presence doesn't leave me when my patience does."

Humor deflates the ego's drama and makes room for grace. Remember: You are not auditioning to be a spiritual superhero. You are learning to be honestly human, filled with God.

A Life That Feels Different From the Inside

Over time, everyday awakening doesn't necessarily make your life look "impressive" from the outside. You may still:

- work the same job,
- live in the same house,
- drive the same car,
- shop at the same store.

But from the inside, life feels different:

- You feel guided instead of alone.
- You feel held instead of constantly on the edge.
- You feel invited instead of pressured.
- You feel more curious and less controlling.
- You find yourself quicker to bless, slower to curse, and more willing to see Christ in unexpected places.

This is what Jesus meant when He talked about the kingdom being "within you." The coordinates of your life may not change, but the climate does. And as that inner climate shifts, people around you will feel it, even if they can't name it. You become quietly luminous. Not because you're trying to shine, but because you're learning to stop blocking the Light that's already there.

* * *

Key Insight

Everyday awakening is not about escaping your ordinary life. It isn't about a change of cars, or house, or jobs...it's a change of heart. It is about inhabiting it with God.

- Prayer becomes awareness, not performance.
- Guidance becomes dialogue, not guessing.
- "Spiritual life" becomes the way you load the dishwasher, sit in meetings, talk to your kids, and drive across town.
- Failure becomes feedback, not final judgment.

You do not have to manufacture the Light. You are learning to recognize it, return to it, and live from it in the middle of your very real, very human days.

Reflection Practice

Building a Life of Quiet Yeses

Name Your "Tiny Altars": Choose 2–3 natural pauses in your day (waking up, doorway, red light, coffee, etc.). For each, write a one-sentence intention like: "When I pour my coffee, I will breathe, 'Thank You for this day.'" "When I walk through a doorway, I will remember, 'I carry Light into this room.'" Put a small reminder where needed (a note, a phone alarm, a symbol).

One Honest Check-In: Sometime midday, pause for 60 seconds and ask: "Where am I right now; scattered, anxious, peaceful, numb?" Don't fix it. Just tell the truth in God's presence. You might add: "Here I am. Meet me here."

Rewrite One Ordinary Moment Think of a daily task you usually rush through or resent (dishes, emails, commuting). Ask: "How could this become a small practice of presence or love?" Maybe it's praying for each person in your inbox...or turning off the radio once a day and driving in silence with God...or blessing each family member while you fold their clothes. Try it once. Notice the difference.

A Nightly Re-Alignment: Before sleep, place a hand over your heart and review your day briefly. "Where today did I remember the Light? "Where did I forget?" Thank God for the moments of awareness. For the other places, simply say: "Thank You that even when I forget You, You do not forget me. I return to You now."

CHAPTER TWENTY-TWO

***

THE REALIZED LIFE

Christ Lives in Me

All along this journey we've been circling one great mystery: *What would it look like to actually live from the Light within...not just believe in it, not just visit it, but live as its expression?*

We've called it awakening, alignment, embodiment, union. Scripture says it in a single line that sounds too good to be ordinary:

"It is no longer I who live, but Christ lives in me." (Galatians 2:20)

Most of us quietly file that verse under *"beautiful but unrealistic."* We assume it belongs only to the spiritual giants, the desert saints, the mystics, the people who speak softly and never seem to sweat.

But Paul was not describing a rare mystical exception. He was describing what happens when a human being: stops trying to fix themselves by willpower alone, stops living as if they are separate from God, and begins to trust that the Living Christ actually dwells within them.

The "realized life" is not a life without problems. It is a life that knows where home is, and keeps returning there until home begins to live through you.

Realization Is Union, Not Promotion

We often imagine "realized" people as spiritually promoted humans: upgraded, advanced, moved to the VIP section of heaven.

But realization is not a promotion. It is union. It is the deep, steady knowing: "I am in Christ, Christ is in me, and nothing, not life or death or anything in between, can undo that."

Realization is not: "Look how spiritual I've become."

Realization is closer to: "I am finally relaxing into what has always been true, and letting that Truth live in me."

A realized person is not someone who has won the spiritual game. It is someone who has surrendered the illusion of playing it alone.

What the Realized Life Is Not

Before we describe what it is, it's helpful to clear what it isn't. A realized life is not:

- A life with no emotions. (Jesus wept. Jesus got tired. Jesus groaned. Jesus rejoiced.)
- A life with no conflict. (He was misunderstood, resisted, and opposed.)
- A life of constant mystical fireworks. (Most of His life looked very... human.)
- A life of religious performance. (He resisted performative spirituality more than anyone.)

And it's definitely not:
- A permanent soft-focus filter,
- a mystical voice,
- and a wardrobe change to all white linen.

If your spirituality makes you less human instead of more, something has gone off course. A realized life is not about floating above reality. It is about moving with reality in God.

The Center of the Realized Life: "Christ in You"

Paul called it: "Christ in you, the hope of glory." (Colossians 1:27) Not just Christ for you. Not just Christ beside you. Christ in you.

The realized life takes this seriously. It begins to shift:

> From: *"I'm trying really hard to be like Jesus"* to *"Jesus, be Yourself in me today."*

From: *"I must manufacture light."* to *"I will stop blocking the Light already here."*

From: *"I live my life for God."* to *"My life is hidden with Christ in God, and I live from that place."*

This doesn't make you passive. It makes you available. You stop white-knuckling your transformation and begin to cooperate with the One who is already at work in you.

Marks of a Heart Living the Realization of the Light Within

Realization is hard to define, but you can often feel its fruit. Here are some of the quiet signs:

Deep Peace in an Un-peaceful World: A person learning to live from this realization still feels waves of fear, sadness, disappointment. But underneath, there is a deeper current of peace that no longer disappears with every storm. They live as if Jesus actually meant it when He said: "My peace I give to you... not as the world gives." (John 14:27)

This doesn't mean they never wobble. It means their *center* is no longer built out of circumstances.

Nonresistance to What *Is* (But Not Passivity): Nonresistance does not mean you never say "no," never confront injustice, or never feel a strong preference. Nonresistance means:

- you stop arguing with reality as if your protest alone could change it,
- you stop living in constant inner "No!" to what already exists,
- you bring what is into the Light and ask, "How can love move here?" instead of, "How do I control everything?"
- you are honest with the truth in hopes of healing instead of hurting someone.

Someone living from this realization can still take strong action. But their action arises from clarity and love, not panic and ego.

You cannot heal what you refuse to see. Nonresistance is the courage to see clearly and then act from union rather than reactivity.

Radiance Without Performance: A person living in harmony with the Light often shines, but not in a "look at me" way. It's more like:

- people feel calmer around them,
- they feel seen instead of judged,
- conversations go deeper without being forced,
- others feel permission to be honest.

This is radiance. Not a spotlight you aim at yourself, but a light that quietly spills from you because you're not so busy defending a false self anymore.

Jesus called it being "salt" and "light." Not loud. Not flashy. Simply present in such a way that: Something about them feels like home."

Compassion and Clarity Together: The more 'realized' a person is, the more they can hold two things at once: fierce clarity about what is true and a tender compassion for those who are still tangled in untruth.

They don't confuse love with enabling. They don't confuse boundaries with rejection.

They can say: "This behavior is not okay," without saying, "You are not okay." Because they have allowed Love to see all of *their* shadows without condemnation, they become less inclined to condemn yours.

Simplicity and Freedom From Drama: As realization deepens, life often becomes simpler, not necessarily on the outside, but on the inside.

- Less obsession with how you're being perceived.
- Less need to be right in every argument.
- Less appetite for drama (even if you notice your ego still occasionally enjoys it).
- More interest in what actually gives life.

The realized life is not boring. It is less cluttered. There is more room for joy, creativity, stillness, and genuine connection because your soul is not constantly running interference.

Humor and Humility: You can't talk about realized people without mentioning humility. The ones who are most full of God tend to be the least impressed with themselves. And they often have a disarming sense of humor.

They can laugh, gently, at their own lingering ego patterns. Not in self-hatred, but in relief: "There I go again. Thank God grace is bigger than my latest episode." Their humility doesn't look like self-loathing. It looks like:

- an ease about their imperfections,
- a quickness to apologize,
- a readiness to listen,
- a refusal to take themselves more seriously than God does.

They are not trying to be "small." They are just clear about who the Source is.

A Nervous System at Peace

We've touched several times on the way science quietly affirms spiritual reality. Research on the nervous system and heart–brain coherence shows:

- When a person lives in chronic fear, resentment, or defensiveness, their nervous system stays in fight-or-flight. Their body is constantly braced.
- When a person repeatedly returns to love, gratitude, trust, and presence, their heart rhythms and brain waves become more ordered and coherent. Their body literally settles into peace.

Realization isn't just a theological idea. Your whole being begins to reflect it. And here's the beautiful part: Regulated nervous systems help regulate other nervous systems.

In neuroscience they call it *co-regulation*. Spiritually, it looks like this:

- You walk into a tense room, and something eases.
- You stay grounded in God's presence, and someone else finds it easier to breathe.
- You choose nonreactivity in a conflict, and another person discovers they don't have to escalate after all.

You may never know the full impact of your inner alignment on the field around you. But it matters. When Paul said, "We are ambassadors of Christ," he wasn't only describing our message. He was describing our presence.

Realized... and Still Becoming

It's important to say this plainly: No one on earth lives in perfect, unbroken realization 24/7. Even the saints had bad days.

The question is not: *"Have I arrived?"*

The question is: *"Am I letting Christ live more freely in me than last year?"* *"Am I returning quicker when I drift?"* *"Am I more available to love, even in hard places?"*

The realized life is both gift and process.

Gift: You are already in union with Christ. You can't earn that.

Process: You are learning to live like it's true, day by day, choice by choice.

Walking Toward Realization (Without Strain)

How do you cooperate with this? Not by gritting your teeth and deciding, "From now on I will be perfectly Christlike." But by growing a simple, steady prayer: "Christ, be Yourself in me today." You can whisper it:

- in the kitchen,
- in the car,
- in a difficult meeting,
- in a moment of temptation,
- in a moment of joy. "

Be Yourself in me" means:

- Love through me.
- See through me.
- Speak through me.
- Forgive through me.
- Rest through me.
- Give wisdom through me.

You are not trying to *imitate* Him from a distance. You are letting Him move from the inside. Add to that a few simple, practical agreements:

- I will pause before reacting.
- I will tell the truth (kindly) instead of hiding.

- I will ask, "What is the loving thing?" even when I don't feel like it.
- I will return when I drift instead of condemning myself.

These are not conditions for God's presence. They are ways of keeping your inner door open.

Living From Light

As realization deepens, the "I" in your sentences slowly shifts.
From: "I have to fix this."..."I have to control this."..."I have to save everyone."

To: "We will walk through this. Christ in me, and me in Christ."..."I am not alone in this room."..."I am an instrument, not the orchestra."

You may still: plan, work hard, lead, create, parent, and build. But underneath, something has changed. The Light is no longer a visitor who comes and goes. It is the One you live from.

You begin to say, with more and more honesty: "It is no longer I who live, but Christ lives in me."

Not as a slogan, but as a lived reality that keeps unfolding.

Final Meditation: Living From Light

Take a few slow breaths. Place a hand over your heart. Let these words rise within you, in your own way:

"Holy One within me, Light of the world, I belong to You. It is not my job to manufacture holiness. It is my joy to make room for You. Be Yourself in me today. Think through my mind. Love through my heart. Speak through my words.

Where I am afraid, be my peace. Where I am stubborn, be my surrender. Where I am weary, be my rest. Where I am closed, be my opening. I offer You my life, ordinary and imperfect, as a place for Your Light to live.

Let my presence become a quiet blessing wherever I go, not because I am great, but because You are here. Christ in me, the hope of glory. So be it. Amen."

Sit for a moment in the stillness that follows. You don't have to feel anything special. You are simply acknowledging what is already true: You are not separate from the Light you seek.

* * *

Key Insight

The realized life is not about becoming spiritual royalty. It is about living from the union that has always been yours:
- "Christ in you, the hope of glory."
- "It is no longer I who live, but Christ lives in me." Realization does not erase your humanity. It heals it.

You are not becoming less "you." You are becoming the truest version of you...the one who has always been held in God.

Reflection Practice

<u>Walking as Light in Real Time</u>

Try the "Be Yourself in Me" Prayer: For the next few days, whisper this short prayer at least three times a day:

- "Christ, be Yourself in me here." Once in a calm moment.
- Once in a stressful moment. Once in a moment of joy.
- Notice what shifts, not necessarily outside, but inside.

Notice One "Realized" Moment Each Day: At night, ask:

"Where today did I briefly live from Light instead of fear?" It might be tiny...a pause before reacting, a kind word, a moment of unexpected peace. Thank God for that moment. These are the seeds of realization.

Practice Nonresistance With One Situation: Name one thing in your life you've been fighting internally: a delay, a limitation, a person, a season. Pray:

"I stop arguing with that this is here. I bring it into Your Light. Show me how love can move in this, instead of just resistance."

You're not surrendering to injustice; you're surrendering your illusion of control.

Bless Your Presence: Place a hand on your chest and say slowly: "Because You live in me, my presence matters more than I know. Let my nervous system be a place of peace. Let my words carry kindness. Let my eyes see with Your Light."

Walk into your next interaction as if that were literally true...because it is.

The realized life is not perfection—it's presence made practical, love made steady, truth made lived. And even here, there is more: the journey continues.

EPILOGUE: THE JOURNEY CONTINUES

The Light That Walks You Home

If you've made it this far, something in you has already answered a call. You may not feel "awakened enough." You may still have questions, doubts, or days that feel heavier than you hoped.

But you are here, reading about Light, considering a different way of being, listening for a Voice that has been whispering to you all along. That is not an accident.

The same Presence that first stirred your heart to say, "There is more," is the Presence that has walked with you through these pages.

You have not just been reading a book. You have been in conversation...with your own soul...with the Spirit of God... with the Light that has always been within you, waiting to be recognized.

This Is Not the End

Books have to end. Journeys don't.

You will close these pages. You'll go back to your real life; to work and bills, to family and friends, to emails, laundry, and news headlines. Nothing may look different on the surface. But *you* are not the same.

- You have seen that awakening is remembering, not earning.
- You have seen that fear is often a story, not a verdict.
- You have seen that the split within you is not your identity, but a wound Love is already healing.
- You have seen that death is not the end of your story.
- You have seen that justice is revelation, not revenge.
- You have seen that eternity is not an endless pause, but an endless unfolding in God.
- You have seen that everyday life can be a sanctuary, if you let it.

You won't "hold onto" all of this perfectly. You're not meant to. You are meant to walk with it...one choice, one moment, one breath at a time.

The Light Has Never Left
There will still be days when:
- the old fear comes back,
- the old story starts playing,
- the old habits tug at you,
- the old questions resurface.

On those days, I hope you will remember this simple truth:

The Light has never left you. You are not starting over. You are only remembering again.

You can always pause, right where you are, and whisper:

> *"Here I am. I feel scattered, tired, unsure...*
> *but I am willing to turn toward the Light again."*

That willingness; even shaky, even small, is enough. You are not carried by the strength of your grip on God. You are carried by the strength of God's grip on you.

You Don't Walk Alone
Wherever you are reading this; in a quiet room, on a lunch break, in a parked car, late at night, you are part of a much larger story. There are others, all over the world, who are also waking up, also wrestling with fear, also daring to believe that Love really is the deepest truth of reality.

You may never meet them on this side of eternity. But you are walking a shared path:
- learning to live from Presence,
- learning to listen to Spirit,
- learning to forgive quickly,
- learning to see Christ in yourself and in others,
- learning to trust that the universe is not hostile ground but holy ground.

You are not weird for wanting more. You are not foolish for hoping that grace is bigger than you were told. You are not naïve for believing that union with God is possible here and now. You are responding to what you were made for.

A Final Blessing

We are living in a pivotal moment—an age where extremes grow louder and hearts grow weary. The path forward is not winning arguments, but meeting at the fulcrum of humility and love—where truth can be spoken without contempt, and difference doesn't cancel compassion.

As you step past these pages and back into your days, I offer you this blessing:

May you remember, in the middle of the most ordinary moments, that you are not separate from the Presence you seek.

May the Holy Spirit, the Breath of God, the inner Counselor, make these truths more real to you than any fear, shame, or lie you've ever believed.

May you discover that stillness is never empty, but filled with the One who loves you.

May your mind be renewed, your nervous system calmed, your heart softened, your body honored, your story re-read in the light of grace.

May you have the courage to step into the flames of transformation when they call, trusting that nothing true about you can be burned away... only what you are not.

May the name of Jesus, the One in whom all Light, Love, and Life are held together, become less of an idea and more of a living reality in you.

May you taste, even now, the joy of knowing that death is not your ending, but a doorway into even more of the Love you are already learning to trust.

And may you walk this earth as a quiet, steady lamp in a world that has forgotten its own Light, not in perfection. But in honest dependence, knowing that every step can be taken in God.

One Last Invitation

Before you go, you might take a moment and simply ask: *"Spirit of Truth and Love, what is the one small thing You are inviting me to live from this book today?"*

Don't try to carry everything. Let one sentence, one picture, one practice rise in your awareness.

- Maybe it's a breath prayer.
- Maybe it's a new way of seeing someone.
- Maybe it's a commitment to tell the truth, to yourself and to God.
- Maybe it's the courage to forgive, or to ask for help, or to step into stillness.

Whatever it is, start there.

The Light that drew you to these pages is the same Light that will meet you in: the next conversation, the next decision, the next sunrise, the next unknown.

This is not goodbye. This is one more turning of the page in a story that does not end:

Light realized...Light remembered...Light lived.

And the journey continues.

About the Author

Jared Richey has served in public education for nearly three decades and writes with one central conviction: the light within us is not imaginary, it is a divine invitation. He believes true transformation is not performance, but awakening: becoming honest, becoming present, becoming love. *Light Realized* was born from a simple longing...to step off the roller coaster of fear and finally live what the soul has always known is possible: peace, clarity, and a life that feels whole.

Jared loves being at home with his family, spending time outdoors, and returning often to stillness...where gratitude grows and perspective is restored. His work is shaped by the belief that life is meant to be lived fully, and that ordinary moments can become doorways into Presence. Jared's hope is that *Light Realized* helps you remember what has been true all along; and gives you simple ways to live it, one day at a time.

Connect with Jared Richey at **light.realized@gmail.com**